Rosemary Stewart's career has been mainly in research and teaching combined for seven years with managing. Her research has covered a wide range of management subjects and of organizations in industry and commerce, local government and the NHS. Her major research interests have been: what managers do, what their jobs are really like and how they differ, management development and management in the National Health Service. She has had two periods of managing: one of five years as the director of the Acton Society Trust, an independent research society and more recently as Dean of Templeton College, Oxford. Doctor Stewart teaches graduate students in management studies at Oxford University and middle and senior managers from many different kinds of organizations. She is the author of *The Reality of Organizations*, also published in this series by Pan Books.

ALSO BY ROSEMARY STEWART
IN PAN BOOKS

The Reality of Organizations

ROSEMARY STEWART

The Reality of Management

SECOND EDITION

PAN BOOKS
LONDON, SYDNEY AND
AUCKLAND

First published 1963 by William Heinemann Ltd
Second edition 1985
This edition published 1986 by Pan Books Ltd,
Cavaye Place, London SW10 9PG
in association with William Heinemann Ltd
9 8 7 6 5
© Rosemary Stewart 1963, 1979, 1985, 1986
ISBN 0 330 29177 7
Printed and bound in Great Britain by
Cox & Wyman Ltd, Reading

Contents

Introduction

This book is addressed to all managers who wish to learn more about their jobs for the practical reason of becoming better managers, and to all students who seek to learn something of the realities of management. It also includes references, and a bibliography that should be useful to the management training officer.

The idea for this book developed during many discussions that followed my visits, as a guest lecturer, to management courses and conferences. These discussions took place with managers at all levels and from many different types of company. They showed two things: first, there are remarkably few books on management, apart from the purely anecdotal, that most managers do not find either too ponderous, or too theoretical, to be readable; secondly, that managers are interested in descriptions of social research into management practice and problems. (Social research is the study of people, both as individuals and in groups.) Therefore, I decided to try to write a book that I hoped managers would find both readable and useful. The material for it comes from two sources: from the research I have done during the last twelve years, during which time I interviewed over 1,500 managers about their work and problems; and from the works of other students of management.

The aim of *The Reality of Management* is to review what has been written about management in practice; to describe some of the results of social research in management which may be of value to the practising manager; and to do so, briefly, clearly and with a minimum use of jargon. Throughout I shall try to show the differences as well as the similarities of managers' jobs. I shall discuss the manager in his setting – which I shall call situation – working in a particular organization with its own distinctive character and problems; in an industry which differs in some ways from others; and in a particular locality and country where the way in which one manages is influenced by local and national traditions.

I should like to express my thanks to the Department of Economics, Massachusetts Institute of Technology, which, by kindly making me a guest from September 1961 to January 1962, gave me the time and the facilities to finish this book. I should also like to thank John H. Smith, lecturer in social science at the London School of Economics and Political Science, for his editorial help.

R.S., 1963

Introduction to the Revised Edition

Seventeen years have passed since this book was written, but I have been surprised on re-reading it to discover how little it dates. Much of the reality of management has remained the same. Inevitably some changes to the book are necessary. Figures and some of the illustrations must be brought up to date. There is new research that is worth telling managers about, even in a short book like this. The effect of social, political and economic changes upon managers requires, in places, a change of emphasis. Two major and related developments must be included. They are not new, but they affect more managers than they did in the early sixties. One is the spread of active unionism to new groups of employees; people strike, or take other industrial action, who would not have done so when this book was first written. The other is the greater importance attached in Western Europe, including the UK to workers' participation in decision-making within the organization.

In many ways it is harder to be a manager in the UK and in some European countries than it was in the early sixties. The manager's right to take decisions without consulting subordinates is more often questioned, even challenged. Hence a different approach to managing is required than that adopted by many managers in the past: an approach that was discussed in the original version of this book, but which has become more essential. It is a change that is especially hard for older managers who are authoritarian by inclination, but many younger managers also complain of the decline in their authority. It is a situation that seems likely to persist, and hence one to which managers will have to adopt.

Many more people think of themselves as managers than when this book was written. Nursing administrators, hospital administrators, park superintendents, farmers, prison governors, headmasters, even bishops, are recognizing that they, too, are managers. To all of them this book is addressed. It is an introduction that seeks to help them to understand and to cope better with the reality that they meet in their working lives. Students of management may also like to read a short introduction before they embark, as they must, on longer and weightier books.

Oxford Centre for Management Studies, 1979.

Introduction to the Second Edition

Many managers' jobs are harder in the mid-eighties than they were in the early sixties when this book was first written or in the late seventies when it was revised. That revision was a minor one. Since then external conditions have changed radically for most managers both in companies and in the public service. A major revision of the book was obviously necessary to describe the reality of management today, although the basics of managing remain the same.

Extensive changes are made in this edition to take account of the following: the shift in Western Europe from full employment to substantial unemployment, increasing world competition, pressures for more cost-effectiveness in public services, the greater awareness of the importance of management in all kinds of organizations, and the growing importance of managing information stemming from developments in computers and related technology. This new edition also takes account of later social research that is relevant to managers.

Any revision must also take account of the change in attitudes to the use of the male pronoun alone. This has been done here by making much greater use of the plural, managers, which in English fortunately has no gender; by the use of he and she; and where a single pronoun is better by occasionally using she rather than he.

Managers are under greater pressures than they were in the past. This makes it even more necessary for them to understand the realities of management and to become better managers. Therefore, a new last chapter has been added to review the common problems facing managers and to suggest how they can be tackled. There is an even greater emphasis in this new edition on making the book helpful to managers, as well as remaining suitable as an introductory text for managerial students. The order of Parts I and II is reversed as the new Part I is of more direct relevance to most managers than the first two chapters of Part II. Managers who read the book for their own guidance rather than as part of a course will probably find Chapters 1, 2, 3, 4, 8, 10 and 11 of most use, particularly 3 and 11.

Typing and retyping a new edition, even on a word processor, is more wearing than dealing with a new book. My most grateful thanks to Ann Bond for her good-humoured perseverance through all the changes, and to Carolyn Jones for her help to Ann in the later stages. I am indebted, too, to my colleagues Dan Gowler and Nick Woodward for suggesting some of the changes that I ought to make, and to Joe Egerton for his energetic and resourceful work in the library and for his suggestions.

Templeton College: The Oxford Centre for Management Studies, 30 April 1985.

Part I

The Job

This section has four chapters. The first looks at the theoretical writing on the manager's functions; then at what research shows about how managers work in practice. The manager's job is divided into making decisions and getting the job done. Each of these is discussed in a separate chapter, with examples from research which should help the manager to make better decisions and to implement them more successfully. The last chapter summarizes research on leadership and what it can tell us about the nature of managers' jobs, and its relevance to the selection and development of managers.

What Does the Manager Do?

What is the manager's job? To ask this question implies that there is a management job; that there are common elements in any management job, whether it is that of a works manager in a small firm in the light-engineering industry, a marketing manager in a medium-sized company selling canned fruit, the chief accountant of a large insurance company, the chief of social services in a local authority, a hospital administrator, a headmaster or a farm manager. Is it possible to separate and define these elements? The first part of this chapter summarizes the traditionally accepted description of the manager's functions. The second part looks at what we know about managers' jobs in practice.

The Manager's Job: Theory

Functions

Henri Fayol in 1908 listed the functions that managers perform. His five-fold classification has been used, with minor modifications, to the present day. First, managers must plan: set objectives, forecast, analyse problems, and make decisions – that is, formulate policy. (Some writers, however, say that 'setting objectives' is the function of the directors. In the broadest sense this is, or should be, true.) Secondly, managers organize: they determine what activities are necessary to achieve the objectives, they classify the work, divide it and assign it to groups and individuals. Thirdly, managers motivate: that is, they inspire their staff to contribute to the purposes of the organization, to be loyal to its aims and to pull their weight in achieving them. Fourthly, managers control what is done by checking performance against the plans. Drucker uses the word 'measurement' instead of 'control'.[1] This is not just a synonym, for it suggests a shift in emphasis from seeing that orders are obeyed to setting objectives and providing the yardsticks for self-control. The idea of control as something imposed upon subordinates is replaced by the idea of guidance and the establishment of standards.

To these four functions, planning, organizing, motivating, and controlling, many authors add coordinating. But this is too general a term to be satisfactorily isolated as an element in the manager's job. Coordination encompasses planning, as in the division of duties between jobs, and also communication if it is to be effective, as well as motivation and control. As Sune Carlson, a Swedish professor of business administration, pointed out in the first major study of what managers actually do: 'The concept of coordinating does not describe a particular set of operations but all operations which lead to a certain result, "unity of action".'[2] Drucker[3] makes an important addition to these major managerial tasks, that of the development of people.

Definitions

The definitions of management are more varied than the descriptions of its functions. Brech defines management as:

1. Drucker, Peter, *People and Performance: The Best of Peter Drucker on Management*, Heinemann, London, 1977, p. 55.
2. Carlson, Sune, *Executive Behaviour: A Study of the Work Load and the Working Methods of Managing Directors*, p. 24, Strombergs, Stockholm, 1951.
3. Drucker, *People and Performance*, op. cit., p. 55.

A social process entailing responsibility for the effective and economic planning and regulation of the operations of an enterprise, in fulfilment of given purposes or tasks, such responsibility involving:

(a) judgement and decision in determining plans and in using data to control performance and progress against plans;
(b) the guidance, integration, motivation and supervision of the personnel composing the enterprise and carrying out its operations.[4]

Barnard in his well-known book *The Functions of the Executive* stresses that:

Executive work is not that of the organization but the specialized work of maintaining the organization in operation.[5]

Robert Heller, a popular writer on management, thinks that any attempt to define the term is doomed to failure. He says:

Any definition of management must be right, because almost any definition must fit something so amorphous and shifting. 'Achieving results through other people' is among the most popular definitions.[6]

Drucker describes management as having three tasks to perform: to fulfil the specific purpose and mission of the organization; to make work productive and the worker achieving; and to manage social impacts and social responsibilities.[7] It is interesting to note the differences between this description in 1977 and that which Drucker gave in *The Practice of Management* in 1954. The third task above was not included in the earlier description. Management in many countries in the world had to be more conscious in the

4. Brech, E. F. L. (ed.), *The Principles and Practice of Management*, Longman, London, 1975, 3rd edition, p. 19.

5. Barnard, Chester, *The Functions of the Executive*, p. 215, Harvard University Press, Cambridge, Mass, 1958 (originally published Oxford University Press, 1938).

6. Heller, Robert, *The Naked Manager*, Barrie and Jenkins, London, 1972.

7. Drucker, *People and Performance*, op. cit., p. 28.

seventies than in the fifties of the social impacts of their activities. That remains true today as managers are under even more pressure to recognize their social responsibilities to the community. Drucker's description of the tasks of management is helpful because it is more concrete than the traditional account of management functions.

The conflicting interests that exist in organizations are now widely recognized by management writers. This in turn affects their descriptions of management's tasks. Kramer, for example, says: '. . . management's task in general . . . is not to widen conflicts but to strike a balance between divergent interests and constantly strive to harmonize them.'[8]

All these definitions can be useful when one considers the nature of the manager's job. But we want a simple definition that can be used when we discuss the manager's job in practice in subsequent chapters. A distinction can be made in the manager's functions between *deciding what to do* and *getting it done*. The manager's job can, therefore, be broadly defined as 'deciding what should be done and then getting other people to do it'. A longer definition would be concerned with how these two tasks are to be accomplished. The first task comprises setting objectives, planning (including decision-making), and setting up the formal organization. The second consists of motivation, communication, control (including measurement), and the development of people. The two tasks are separated for convenient analysis, but in practice they may often overlap. For instance, a manager who wishes to reach a decision acceptable to subordinates, and therefore more easily implemented, may include them in the process of decision-making. The increasing importance attached to participation may make it essential to do so.

It is not necessary to consider here which policy decisions are made by the Board and which by management. Practice varies from one company to another. It is sufficient for our discussion of the manager's job that all managers must be concerned, to some extent, with policy-making.

8. Kramer, H. E. 'The Philosophical Foundation of Management Rediscovered', *Management International Review*, 1975, Vol. 15/2–3.

The Manager's Job: Practice

The traditional account of management functions: planning, organizing, motivating, controlling and coordinating, is very broad. It is still repeated in many management textbooks, but what is its practical value? One test of this is whether it is a guide for the selection and the training of managers. To a limited extent it is. To know, for instance, that managers plan and motivate can help us to eliminate some people: 'He would never make a manager because he is too muddle-minded ever to be able to plan anything' or 'He is too retiring to be able to motivate anybody'. But the usefulness of such analysis is limited because the job of the manager is so varied. In one job it is important to be good at planning, in another it may be only a very minor part of the job. Even the ability to motivate others matters much more in some jobs than in others. Another test of the practical value of these five categories is whether they help managers to review how well they do their job. They are too broad and too abstract to be of any real use for this purpose.

Differences in Managerial Jobs

Traditional accounts of managing emphasize the common aspects. It is important to do so, but it is also important to understand the very wide differences that exist between managerial jobs. These are ignored in most books on management. Research into the nature of managers' jobs has highlighted many of the less obvious differences, but even the obvious ones are often ignored in traditional management writing. It *is* different to manage in a small organization compared with a large one, though adaptable managers can make the transition. The job of coke-ovens manager in a steel mill has few similarities with that of a management services manager in an insurance broking firm, because of the differences in function, in industry and in the kind of people who work in the two companies. The firm's competitive position also affects what it is like to be a manager. Those who work in companies that are struggling in a highly competitive and rapidly changing industry have very different jobs from those who are managers in a company in a slow moving industry where it has a major share of the market. Above all a rapid rate of change can transform a manager's job, as many managers have found out.

Research has begun to clarify some of the differences between managerial jobs in the same organization, other than the generally recognized ones of level and function.[9] One is the pattern of the day. The writer identified four types of pattern that characterize different jobs.[10] One of these patterns, which is called Project, is quite unlike the more usual fragmented day. The work permits, and requires, long periods of uninterrupted activity. Naturally, it suits some people better than the more normal disjointed day, while others are much happier being hectically busy. This is an example of a difference in the nature of managerial work that is rarely, if ever, taken into account in a job specification. Another difference that will not be found in a job description is the extent of exposure that the jobholder must bear. In some jobs the holder who performs badly can be clearly identified: that is an exposed job. In others the individual's contribution to failures cannot be identified: the manager in that job is not exposed.

Who the manager has to work with also helps to determine what the job is like. Managerial jobs differ in the types and difficulty of the contacts that have to be made. They thus make different demands upon the social skills of the jobholder.[11] A change from a job with one type of contacts to another with very different ones can make difficult and unexpected demands upon the manager: 'unexpected' because this is another characteristic of a job that is not adequately recognized.

No adequate selection and training can take place unless these differences are appreciated. 'A good manager can

9. Readers who are interested in understanding the differences between managerial jobs are referred to Mintzberg, Henry, *The Nature of Managerial Work*, Harper and Row, New York, 1973, Chapter 5; and Stewart, Rosemary, *Contrasts in Management: A Study of Different Types of Managers' Job: their Demands and Choices*, McGraw-Hill (UK), Maidenhead, 1976.

10. Stewart, ibid., Chapter 4.

11. Stewart, ibid., Chapter 2.

manage anything' is a common statement. Yet it is a belief that is rarely put into practice in most organizations. Changes between functions in the same organization are often restricted. Moves between companies after the age of forty are also uncommon, though it is easier in some occupations than in others. Two reasons are usually given for this immobility: one, the amount of technical knowledge required, particularly at the lower levels, and, two, the need to know one's way round in the company. Learning the ropes is an essential part of a new manager's job. Most large organizations are unwilling to pay those over the age of thirty while they acquire this knowledge unless they have some needed expertise to offer. In general, therefore, management does not behave as if it believes that a good manager can manage anything.

The idea that a good manager can manage anything should be nearer to the truth for top management, where the technical content is lowest and where the tone is set by the managing director. Even there, the kinds of people who have to be managed and the types of problem that have to be resolved can be so diverse that they require different abilities and, therefore, different people. This was highlighted by Kotter, reporting on his study of fifteen general managers, who said that:

> We have found that the type of GM job, the nature of the business, and the nature of the corporation involved can all shape GM job demands in important ways that can require different kinds of GMs. For example, somewhat different types of people seem to be needed depending upon whether the job context is young or old, small or large, performs well or is in need of a 'turn-around'.[12]

Kotter deplored the 'I can do anything' syndrome. He found that the general managers that he studied had 'little conscious awareness just how specialized their skills, their knowledge, and their relationships really were'.[13]

12. Kotter, John, *The General Managers*, The Free Press, New York, 1982.
13. ibid., p. 142.

Differences in What Managers Do

Kotter found that the jobs of the general managers whom he studied differed. He also found that the managers did their jobs differently, but this could have been explained by the distinctive nature of each job. However, studies by Stewart show that managers in similar jobs also differ in what they do.[14] Each manager does the job in his or her own way. This can be seen quite simply by comparing the amount of time spent with different kinds of contacts. One manager may be downward-focused, spending most time with subordinates. Another may concentrate much more upon work with other departments. Yet another may be primarily outward-focused, spending a lot of time with people outside the organization. Some managers get their satisfaction out of performing on a larger stage than their own company and, therefore, make the most out of the opportunities that public relations give them to do so. In the more constrained jobs managers emphasize some aspects and neglect others. In the more flexible jobs two people in similar jobs can spend much of their time doing different kinds of work. All managers' jobs are sufficiently flexible to permit one manager to choose to do different kinds of work from another manager in a similar job. But this choice is often unconscious: many managers do not realize that the job could be done differently from the way that they do it.

Managers do their jobs differently partly because they see them differently. Each manager starting in a new job will have a distinctive view of what needs doing. He or she will focus attention on particular problems and not notice others. Further, managers differ in what they enjoy doing and in what they are good at, and these factors also will influence how they spend their time.

The opportunities for choice that exist in managerial jobs need to be recognized by the individual manager and by all those concerned with the selection, appraisal and training of managers. So does the fact that few managers adequately

14. Stewart, Rosemary, *Choices for the Manager*, McGraw-Hill (UK), Maidenhead, 1982.

recognize this choice, either in their own jobs or in those of their subordinates. The simile of finding a round peg to fit a round hole is quite unsuited to the task of selecting a manager. There will always be more things in any managerial job than a particular jobholder has the time, ability or inclination to do. Hence the task of selection is to find the person who will make the choices that are most needed at a particular time, taking into account the choices made by boss, subordinates and fellow members of the management team.

Similarities in Managerial Work

A detailed study of what managers do in practice was made shortly after the last war by Sune Carlson,[15] who looked at the workload and working methods of nine Swedish managing directors. It was a detailed study of how they spent their time for four weeks. Carlson's findings have been confirmed by subsequent research in the US and the UK.[16] All studies show that the manager's day is typically fragmented: most managers have to switch their attention frequently from one person to another. The research gives a picture of a hectic manager's day that contrasts with the theorists' calm description of a manager who plans, organizes and controls.

Much managerial work is necessarily fragmented, but a study by the author found that managers also fragment their work more than they need. This is rarely a conscious choice. Indeed, when managers keep a record of what they do, they are often shocked to discover the extent of fragmentation. Some of them then resolve to try and organize their work so as to give a period of uninterrupted time for concentration. One way they find of doing this is to attach less importance to being constantly available to other people.

15. Carlson, Sune, *Executive Behaviour*, op. cit.
16. Mintzberg, Henry, *The Nature of Managerial Work*, op. cit. A good summary of the research evidence available up to 1972 on managerial work in practice, as well as contributing an interesting, and original, analysis of the roles that managers have to play. A description of how 160 middle and senior managers in different organizations spent their time during four weeks is given in Stewart, Rosemary, *Managers and Their Jobs, A Study of the Similarities and Differences in the Ways Managers Spend Their Time*, Macmillan, London, 1967; Pan, 1969.

Subsequent studies also confirmed Carlson's finding of the large amount of time that managers spend with other people. Most managers spend three-quarters or more of their time with others, and it is only in rather specialized and backroom jobs that the time may drop to about 50 per cent. Managers work with other people more than many of them realize – their estimates tend to be lower than a record of how they actually spend their time.[17] However, the studies have been done in Europe and the USA, and there may be cultural differences in the extent to which managers prefer writing to talking.

Carlson used the phrase 'administrative pathologies' to describe how his managing directors' actions differed from their views of what was efficient behaviour. He found that they tended to regard their outside activities, which took up to half their time, as a temporary burden, and hence not to plan their work to allow for them. He also found that these chief executives were rarely alone and undisturbed in their offices for periods of more than about ten minutes at a time.

The better our understanding of what managerial work is really like, the better we shall be able to select and train people to perform it well. We need to be able to generalize realistically about the nature of managerial work. The research that has been done can help us to do so. It has made us more aware, for example, of the political nature of many managers' jobs. Traditionally, attention has been focused upon the management of subordinates, but increasingly managers in many jobs have to be skilful at managing relations with people in other departments and outside the organization. Such relations often require political skill: the recognition of conflicts of interests and the ability to enlist support to further one's own job objectives. Some people may shy at the word 'political', and reject the idea that it may apply to their own jobs. Yet, as Leonard Sayles, in an illuminating book on managerial behaviour in practice, has written:

Perhaps the most important lesson the manager can learn concerns the nature of modern organizations. Most Americans and

17. Stewart, Rosemary, *Contrasts in Management*, op. cit., p. 95.

West Europeans are brought up to believe that consensus and unity are an essential ingredient for any successful political, social or economic institution. But this firm belief in oneness does not square with the facts. Companies, like all large organizations, have built-in divisions, and even in the proverbial 'long-run' they tend not to be eliminated. The manager must anticipate that more than one team will be playing in his organization and not find this immoral or upsetting.[18]

Happily, managers without political skills, or those who consider them distasteful, can still find jobs where such skills are not required. One of the great advantages of understanding more about the differences in managerial work is that the match between the individual and the job can be improved.

Traditional accounts of management suggest that managing is an analytical, logical and ordered process. These accounts make managers feel guilty about their own often chaotic days. Research shows that managing is a much more human activity. Many managers, even senior ones, spend much of their time in a whirl of activity, switching their attention every few minutes from one person and subject to another. They rely and – given the brevity of many of their activities – have to rely upon the habits they have developed and upon their intuition. They choose, often unconsciously, from among all the things that they might do those that catch their attention and that they enjoy doing. Nearly all their time is spent with other people, trying to find out what is happening, trying to persuade others to cooperate and less often trying to decide what ought to be done. In many managerial jobs they will need to know how to trade, bargain and compromise. The more senior they are, the more political will be the world in which they live. They will need to secure allies and to avoid creating enemies, or if they do, to gain enough power to make them harmless. The dangers that this picture of management poses to managers who are trying to be effective, and what they can do about it, are discussed in the last chapter.

18. Sayles, Leonard R., *Managerial Behaviour: Administration in Complex Organizations*, McGraw-Hill, New York, 1964, pp. 140–1; and Prentice-Hall, Englewood Cliffs, NJ, 1982.

SUMMARY

In the first half of this chapter we considered the traditional writings on the nature of the manager's job and found that, although terminology differs, there is broad agreement that a manager plans, organizes, motivates and controls. There is disagreement about whether 'coordination' is *a* function of management or a general term for *the* function of a manager. We decided upon a simple definition of management: 'deciding what should be done and then getting other people to do it'. The deciding may, of course, involve those who should implement the decisions. Both decision-making and implementation require organization, which we discuss in Part II.

So much for theory. When we turned to what is known about the manager's work in practice, we found that research into what managers do gives a different picture from traditional accounts of the functions of a manager. The reality of management is less planned, orderly, rational, or objective than these suggest. Most managers spend their time in brief, fragmented activities, switching every few minutes from one person or problem to another. They talk or listen for three-quarters or more of the day. Managing is, even more than most managers realize, working with other people. The implications of what managers typically do for the individual manager are considered in the last chapter.

Managers' jobs vary so much that the statement that 'a good manager can manage anything' is not true. The similarities of managers' jobs have been over-emphasized: the differences are many and important. We need, and with the help of research can make, some useful generalizations about managerial work, but we need to understand the differences, too. There are differences both in jobs and in what individual managers do. Managers in similar jobs can and do concentrate on different aspects of the job and so spend their time in different ways.

2

Making Decisions

Decision-making in industry is a popular subject for discussion and research. Recognizing that the wrong decision may cost thousands, sometimes even millions, of pounds, top management is searching for ways of improving its score of bull's-eyes. Nor need it look for people who are keen to help by such varied methods as modelling decisions, using techniques to aid creativity and by the use of business games as a means of training in decision-taking. Decision-making, like organization, has attracted a crowd of research workers from different disciplines. These look at the problems of making decisions from their own points of view and make their own contributions to our still limited knowledge of the subject. It would take too long to try to summarize here all these different and sometimes highly theoretical approaches to theories of decision-making.[1] Instead we shall discuss some of the simpler things that are now known about the process of decision-making in practice.

1. A wide coverage of the subject is given in Cooke, Steve and Slack, Nigel, *Making Management Decisions*, Prentice-Hall Int., London 1984.

Setting the Sights

Decision-making in industry is made simpler if management sets the boundaries within which the business is to operate. These boundaries are established by defining the objectives, which should be generally understood, whether implicitly or, preferably, explicitly. Writing them down can help to clarify them still further. One of the values of so defining objectives is that it will distinguish them from management beliefs, which may be shown to have no present purpose. Out-dated beliefs tend to continue in any organization. In the armed services it used to be known as 'Generals always fight the last war', but it is just as true in business.

Management beliefs and attitudes are likely to have an important influence on both the type of decision that is made and the speed with which a decision is reached and implemented. Some decisions may never be made because they are not in accord with management's beliefs and priorities. Others may not be implemented, or their implementation long delayed, because management, although it pays lip service to the importance of doing so, does not really believe in their value. An example of this, which is all too frequent, is the delay in implementing plans for the development of future managers.

A few companies publish broad objectives, reflecting their corporate philosophy. This is more common in America than in Britain. Where it is done, the aim is to describe the values that should underlie management decisions. Two examples are given below, one American and one British. Both incorporate the idea of different stakeholders in the company, although they do not use that term. Profit is only one of the objectives and the aim is not maximum profit. Both examples are taken from companies, but an equivalent statement of objectives is a useful guide to decision-making in any kind of organization.

The American company, Hewlett-Packard, is in the electronics industry. It first published its corporate objectives in 1957 and has modified them since from time to time. Those given below are taken from the booklet published in May 1979.

HEWLETT-PACKARD OBJECTIVES

1. PROFIT

   Objective: To achieve sufficient profit to finance our company growth and to provide the resources we need to achieve our other corporate objectives.

2. CUSTOMERS

   Objective: To provide products and services of the greatest possible value to our customers, thereby gaining and holding their respect and loyalty.

3. FIELDS OF INTEREST

   Objective: To enter new fields only when the ideas we have, together with our technical, manufacturing and marketing skills, assure that we can make a needed and profitable contribution to the field.

4. GROWTH

   Objective: To let our growth be limited only by our profits and our ability to develop and produce technical products that satisfy real customer needs.

5. OUR PEOPLE

   Objective: To help HP people share in the company's success which they make possible; to provide job security based on their performance; to recognize their individual achievements; and to help them gain a sense of satisfaction and accomplishment from their work.

6. MANAGEMENT

   Objective: To foster initiative and creativity by allowing the individual great freedom of action in attaining well-defined objectives.

7. CITIZENSHIP

   Objective: To honor our obligations to society by being an economic, intellectual and social asset to each nation and each community in which we operate.

Each objective is followed by an explanation and elaboration.

Glacier Metal in the UK was for many years well known for its much studied social experimentation.[2] It developed a

2. The classic publication was Jaques, Elliot, *Changing Culture of a Factory*, Tavistock Publications, London, 1951.

detailed, written Company Policy Document, notable for its
attention to relations between members of the organization
and the promotion of the well-being of each member.[3]
This document includes the following statement of company
objectives:

C   Achievement of the Purpose of the Company
cl   The purpose of the members employed by the Company is
      the continuity of a working community, the conditions of
      which will promote the physical and mental well-being of
      members and, taking into account all possible circumstances,
      will provide them with the highest possible return for work
      done. The purpose of the members in this respect is consis-
      tent with the legal purpose of the Company as set out in the
      Memorandum of Association dated the 6th December 1935,
      in that both will be achieved by:

cl.1 Ensuring that the Company is able to maintain a high posi-
      tion in the competitive market by reason of its standards
      of price, quality and service to customers. This involves
      research, development and achievement of high technical
      and organizational efficiency.
cl.2 Providing such dividends for its shareholders as will repre-
      sent a reasonable and fair return for their capital investment.
cl.3 Ensuring that every member is paid at a level consistent
      with the role into which he contracted, and that he gets a
      level of work consistent with his capacity, if such work is
      available.
cl.4 Providing reserves sufficient to safeguard the Company and
      all who work within it.
cl.5 Providing the maximum practicable facilities for the health,
      safety and well-being of all members employed by the Com-
      pany.

Such corporate objectives may not be formally set down or
even formulated. Whether they are or not, more specific
objectives will also be needed in any kind of organization. A
company may set, for example, very specific objectives for

3. Brown, Wilfred, 'Company Policy Document', *Exploration in Management*, Appendix II, Heinemann, London, 1960.

the type of product to be manufactured and the markets to be aimed at, such as making high quality shoes. Such specific product objectives are more likely to be found in small and medium-sized companies and in bigger companies in the capital goods industries.

In a large and diverse group of companies the product market objectives may be very general, such as keeping in the consumer-goods industries, or there may even be no limitation on the type of goods to be manufactured. A company that has no product objectives to guide its investment – usually where it has expanded by the acquisition of other firms – must establish other objectives, such as a test of profitability. A common example is a particular return on capital.

Recognizing the Limitations

The objectives are the boundaries that management sets on its freedom of decision. They establish the kind of things that management can do and those that are outside its objectives. There are also other limitations on the freedom to make decisions, but these are not self-imposed, although, in an indirect way, they may be the result of previous decisions. The first of these limitations is shortages of money, staff, and materials. Many business decisions will, therefore, mirror the economist's definition of 'the application of scarce means to alternative ends'. One of the advantages of large-scale organizations is that they are often less limited by shortages of money or staff. The second, and often stringent, limitation on managers' freedom of decision is that imposed by outside agencies, such as the government or trade unions. A third limitation comes from people's attitudes, which we shall be discussing in the next chapter on 'Getting the Job Done'.

The opposition of individual managers may mean that a decision is never reached, or, if it is, the project may flounder through lack of support. For instance, the support of the general sales manager for a proposed new product is probably essential to the success of the sales campaign. The opposition of the rank and file may also mean that a decision can never be successfully implemented. The nature and strength of opposition must be taken into account before a decision is reached. Many limitations are not absolute bars to particular decisions. They may be surmountable. Often more important, they may be anticipated and prevented from becoming a limitation. Organizations are not only subject to the economic, political and social environments within which they operate. They may also be able to partially shape their environment. Political lobbyists are well aware of that!

Analysing Decision-making

The ways in which decisions are made vary from one company to another, even from one part of an organization to another. There are differences in who is involved in reaching a decision, in the process by which this is done and in whether it is recorded. These differences are greater in companies than in the public services, where there are rules governing decision-making, but in any organization its culture and the style of the chief executive will affect the ways in which decisions are taken. In one company nearly all important decisions are made by a group of managers; in another individual managers will often decide on their own. The difference between these two methods is greatest at the top. In one company there will be an active top management committee which takes the major decisions; in another the managing director will take many of these decisions, possibly after consulting senior staff. The latter is more possible in small companies, or larger ones with a simple technology and a stable environment. The decision may, or may not, be based on an agreed document or recorded in any form. In some companies there may never be a formal decision, but an understanding on which instructions are based. The latter, like the bare recording of a decision, may later lead to confusion about exactly what was agreed.

In looking at decision-making it is helpful to trace a logical sequence as a guide to the steps that should be carried out in reaching a decision. Before a decision is made, three things should be done. In simple decisions these stages may be passed through very quickly. First, the reasons for taking a decision must be formulated. This can be done by defining a problem that is to be solved. At this stage it is vital to ask the right questions, otherwise the decision may be the right answer to the wrong question. Second, the nature of the problem must be analysed. Third, the alternative solutions must be examined, together with their possible consequences. The correctness of these preliminary stages will have great influence on the validity of the final decisions.

How these steps should be carried out, and what effect they can have on the correctness of the final decision, may be illustrated by an examination of a question that many companies have to consider at some time: 'whether to produce a new product and, if so, which new product?' This, like most decisions in business, is not a single decision. Usually there are a group of related decisions, or one major decision that entails many subsidiary ones. If top management is considering launching a new product, the first step is to analyse why it wants to do so. The analysis might show, for example, that a competitor's new product is capturing some of the market; that the company has surplus production capacity; or that the sales force is underemployed at some time of the year. One or more of these may be the reasons why management wants to introduce a new product. The definition of the problem may show that what is required is not a new product but, say, a more interesting selling campaign for existing products. We shall assume, however, that the definition of the problem shows that a new product is required. We now pass to the second stage, analysing the nature of the problem, which tells us the kind of new product that is required. The analysis indicates that the new product must meet two needs: diversification and the full utilization of a selling force that at present sells one seasonal product. Therefore, the new product must have a different sales peak from that of the present one.

The first and second stages are now complete; a new product is required to meet two needs. The next stage is the examination of possible solutions against the background of general company objectives. One solution may be found to require the recruitment of new specialists; another may need a heavy capital outlay; another may mean entering a market that suffers from great fluctuations in demand; and yet another may be strongly opposed by the general sales manager, whose cooperation will be needed to launch the new product on the market. Drucker suggests the four following criteria for deciding which is the best of the alternative solutions: the risk involved related to the expected gain; the amount of effort required; the timing, especially whether a dramatic change is desirable or if a slow, one-step-at-a-time approach is more suitable; and the availability of resources, particularly of human abilities.[4]

Each solution may be found to have advantages and disadvantages. If time allows, some of these can be explored further. But even a thorough examination will usually leave imponderables, such as reactions of competitors or the amount and timing of likely market fluctuations on the product. Management will then have to decide which seems to be the best of the alternatives. Before it decides to go ahead on the selected solution, it will need to consider whether the possible advantages are worth the cost and risks. A negative decision – not to do anything at present – may seem the wisest one. A close balance of advantages and disadvantages may be tipped by the thought of the effort necessary and the disruption that would be caused.

Listing criteria for judging between alternative solutions suggests that the decision-makers will then weigh these up and reach a decision. But often it is not that easy, because they may have different opinions. They may disagree about what they want to happen or about what is likely to happen. The example given of a new product is more likely to arouse disagreements about the latter than the former. Such disagreements are easier to resolve than more fundamental ones about what is wanted. The price of disagreement is likely to be inaction or a compromise. The alternatives include agreeing to accept a majority decision or giving one person the power to decide when there is no agreement. What actually happens may depend upon any rules that exist for dealing with disagreements, or upon the relative force of different personalities to carry their own preferences. In more

4. Drucker, Peter F., *The Practice of Management*, pp. 320–1, Heinemann, London, 1955, and Harper and Bros, New York, 1954.

autocratically run organizations the chief executive will decide. But in many organizations, whether private enterprise or public service, the chief executive will, as one managing director put it: 'be able to get away a few times with taking dictatorial decisions, particularly if I prove to be right, but most of the time I have to persuade my staff that the decision is in their best interests, and preferably that the decision was originally their idea'.

Many managers say that they do not have time for careful preliminary investigations. This can be a dangerous half-truth. Sometimes a quick decision is vital, and often it may not be possible to find out all the available facts, but speed is rarely the primary requirement. The old proverb, 'more haste less speed', is often applicable.

Some managers dislike the idea of analysing decisions. In the business world where so much is uncertain, flair, they hold, is more important than logic. Many decisions must rest on a judgement of the relative importance of unknown factors. This is true but it is still necessary to define the problem and to seek to reduce the uncertainties in identifying possible solutions.

The analysis of decisions is one way to try and improve their content. A quite different approach, which can be pursued at the same time, is to try and improve the quality of the original ideas. This matters more for some decisions than for others, more for many marketing decisions than for most personnel decisions. The Americans especially have worried about what they call 'creativity'. One of the techniques to encourage creativity is 'brain-storming', which, it is hoped, will produce new ideas. A group of people are asked to throw out any ideas on a particular subject or problem. These are all recorded, but not discussed at the brain-storming session, the sole purpose of which is to produce new ideas.

Research on Decision-making

The traditional economist's picture of the businessman is of a rational being who, under the pressure of competition, carefully weighs the costs of one action against another and is preoccupied with marginal costs and marginal utility.

Managers, even though they may consider this description of business behaviour to be too academic, will probably still stress the rational element in their decisions – although they may allow that the decisions made by others are often not as objective as they should be. Some economists, along with sociologists and psychologists, are interested in studying how decisions are made in practice.

In many decisions, including investment ones, a number of studies show that hopes, wishes and internal politics play an important part. The element of uncertainty enables expectations of the results of the decision to be biased in accordance with wishes. Cost estimates, for instance, may be too optimistic. Some of these biases may be unconscious; others may be consciously manipulated by managers who want a particular decision to be taken. One study even reports the following statement: 'In the final analysis, if anybody brings up an item of cost we haven't thought of, we can balance it by making another source of savings tangible'.[5] The influence of wishes may also work retrospectively, so that the reasons given for failures may be quite different from the reality, although these reasons are widely accepted as facts. Management's wishes in decision-making may prevent an objective assessment of the value of a proposed project and, if it fails, also prevent an objective assessment – often any assessment at all – of why it failed. This points to a need for looking carefully at even generally accepted 'facts'.

One lesson that comes out of research is that decision-making must be seen as a political process. Pettigrew[6] has given a detailed account over time of the political influences affecting a decision as to which computer to buy. Managers can and should strive to improve the logic of their decisions. It is all too easy to define the problem wrongly or too narrowly, or to plump for the wrong solution. But good logic is not enough. A manager also needs to be alert to the political aspects of decision-making. Political activity is likely when a decision

5. Cyert, R. M., Dill, W. R. and March, J. G., 'The Role of Expectations in Business Decision Making', *Administrative Science Quarterly*, Vol. III, No. 3, p. 340, December 1958.

6. Pettigrew, Andrew M., *The Politics of Organizational Decision-Making*, Tavistock, London, 1973.

affects the distribution of resources and the relative strength and status of different individuals and groups. The arguments that are put forward are likely to be coloured by the different interests affected by the decision.

Research also suggests that the description we gave of the stages in decision-making may, like the economist's models, bear little resemblance to actual business behaviour; rather it is a useful tool for checking the validity of one's reasons or for discovering what has gone wrong. According to William J. Gore, reporting on some research in the USA:

> . . . the traditional idea that a decision is an event stemming from a build-up of facts and is itself a choice between alternatives, very seldom happens. Even in what might be called forced choice situations there may be no deliberate choice. In fact it seems tenable to hold that most decisions are not aggressive choices, and that by their nature they cannot be, for the crux of a decision is not the choice between alternatives but the identification of the costly invisible consequences of such a choice and fabrication of a choice which tiptoes its way through them without setting any of them off.[7]

Decision-making at Different Levels

In some interesting research[8] Norman Martin looked at the differences between decisions at four different levels of management in a large American manufacturing company. He found that the decision situation differed in a number of ways between the levels. By 'decision situation' Martin meant the whole range, from the preliminary stages, through the actual decision and implementation, to verification of the correctness or incorrectness of the decision.

The main differences he discovered were in the length of the time perspective, the amount of continuity and the degree of uncertainty. Decisions at the higher levels have as one

7. In a paper prepared for the Acton Society Trust's annual conference, 1960.
8. 'Differential Decisions in the Management of an Industrial Plant', *Journal of Business*, Vol. 29, No. 4, pp. 249–60, October 1956. (Copyright 1956, University of Chicago.)

would expect a longer time perspective. From first inquiry to verification of the decision took less than two weeks in 97.7 per cent of the shift foreman's decision situations; 68 per cent of the department foreman's decisions situations were completed within two weeks; 54.2 per cent of the division superintendent's; and only 3.3 per cent of the works manager's. Half the works manager's decision situations lasted over a year; 4.3 per cent of the division superintendent's; 1.5 per cent of the department foreman's; and none of the shift foreman's. This shows the striking difference in distant-time perspective between the works manager and the other three levels of management. Decisions at the higher levels tended to be discontinuous, as one would expect with a long time span. There were sometimes wide gaps between the different parts of the decision situation, partly due to the manager having delegated part of the process of carrying through a decision to his subordinates. At the lower levels all the stages tended to follow each other without a time interval, or with only a short one.

The decisions at the lower levels were much more clear cut. What had to be done was more easily seen, it usually had to be done quickly and there was less uncertainty about the result than at higher levels. At the higher levels the decision situation was much more indefinite; the time within which action should be taken was often indeterminate, as it could depend upon the judgement of the total situation; what should be done was often difficult to decide because there were so many elements of uncertainty in the decision. Dr Martin's research suggests that the differences in the nature of the decisions are not evenly spaced from one management level to another. There is much greater change between some levels.

In his study the main division was between the works manager and the division superintendent. Usually the principal cleavage line between types of decisions is likely to be between the top manager(s), both of a company and of an establishment, and the managers below. This would help to explain the difficulty many companies have in finding enough good top managers. Many middle managers may not be able to cope satisfactorily with the much more indeterminate decisions at top-management level.

Training in Decision-making

Differences in the nature of decisions at different management levels have important implications for recruitment, training and promotion. Before a management post is filled, the types of decision that have to be taken should be known. The personality characteristics and the training that a manager will need to cope satisfactorily with indeterminate decisions are likely to be different from those required for decisions made in a short time span about concrete situations. The pace of decisions will also impose demands. Some managers will relish the frequent and rapid decision-taking that characterizes the job of editor of a daily paper. Others may find it too stressful and be more suited to the relatively leisurely pace of a monthly magazine.

The principal difficulty in training for decision-making is to give young managers experience in taking different types of decisions. One of the main arguments used in favour of considerable delegation is that it develops the ability to make decisions. Hence a flat organization, with a small number of management levels, should give more opportunity for decision-making at all levels. Some companies give their young managers experience of top-management decisions by putting them in charge of semi-autonomous units. Then they can feel that it is their business and its success or failure their responsibility. Such training is popular with those senior managers who believe strongly that managers learn by doing and, above all, by their mistakes.

A variety of methods are used in management education to try to improve the quality of decisions. There is broad education about the environment within which the organization operates. This can help managers to understand the factors that may be relevant to their decisions. Most effort in management education has been spent devising methods to help managers to analyse problems and to evaluate solutions. The case method is one way of helping managers to do so. The business game is another. It has the advantage of including time pressures and simulating real life by including an element of chance. Managers can be taught how to model decisions so as to evaluate uncertainties and to examine the effects of making different assumptions. These are all methods aimed at improving the rationality of decisions, but less commonly some management trainers seek to improve managers' sensitivity to the political aspects of decisions and their skills in handling these. All these methods, it can be argued, are divorced from reality, so that managers may behave differently from how they would in their own jobs. The risks of being wrong are less and so are the pressures from other parties to the decision. Most importantly, one does not have to live with the decision. Such methods can be a useful supplement to what the manager can learn on the job, but the right kinds of job experience remain an irreplaceable training ground for decision-taking.

SUMMARY

Management can improve the standard of its decision-making in a number of ways by:

1. Clearly defining the objectives of the business, thus setting the boundaries within which decisions will be made. If the objectives are well-known, it will lessen the danger of out-dated management beliefs having an influence on decisions. Two examples of published corporate objectives showed that these were much wider than the pursuit of profit, though that was a condition of achieving the others.
2. Recognizing the limitations that exist and affect its freedom of decision. These limitations stem from the political and social background, from competition and economic scarcities and from people's attitudes.
3. Analysing decision-making in stages to make certain that it has formulated the reasons for taking a decision and defined the problem to be solved; analysed the nature of the problem; and examined the alternative solutions and their possible consequences.
4. Being suspicious of the argument that there is no time for such an analysis.
5. Being aware of the extent to which hopes, wishes and internal politics prejudice its decisions.

The types of decision made at different levels of management are qualitatively different. The contrast in the length of time, the discontinuity and the indeterminacy of decisions at senior levels, compared to those lower down, points to the problems of selecting and training top managers who can cope satisfactorily with these types of decision. Management education can contribute to improving the analysis of problems and their possible solutions but cannot substitute for experience in a job that needs such decisions. The best training is responsibility for managing a small subsidiary.

3

Getting the Job Done

The second part of managers' jobs is getting things done through people. To do so successfully, managers must solve three different types of problem: those of organization, communication and cooperation. First they must allocate and coordinate the work efficiently. They must decide what to delegate, to whom, and how much. They must also decide how far they wish to spell out responsibilities, defining in detail what they want done. Their decision will be influenced partly by the nature of the organization, partly by their managerial philosophy and partly by their assessment of the capabilities and personalities of subordinates. They will need to know whether the work is done satisfactorily, hence what forms of control to use. Again they will be influenced by their own attitudes to management and by their judgement of subordinates. Some managers feel most comfortable with a close control, so that they know what is happening all the time; some may prefer to encourage their subordinates to check their own performance against mutually agreed standards.

Even where managers decide on their own what needs doing, they must still convey this to their subordinates and enlist their cooperation in doing it. Unfortunately some managers are not aware that either may cause a problem.

Their attitude to implementation may be summed up as 'one gives one's subordinates an order and they carry it out'. Many difficulties come from a failure to recognize the importance of clear communication and willing cooperation. Any manager has to be concerned with both, although the forms of communication and methods of obtaining cooperation may vary to some extent, depending upon the characteristics of both the manager and the managed. A foreman on a construction site talking to a labourer, for instance, will use a different language and a somewhat different approach from that of the managing director of a chemical firm talking to scientific colleagues.

The importance of effective communication and willing cooperation is often most underrated by those managers who still attach primary importance to their technical role, whether as engineers, chemists, accountants or nurses. Such managers may only learn slowly and painfully that people often misunderstand and may be suspicious of the manager's intentions; therefore, implementation will go more smoothly and speedily if the manager takes time to explain what is wanted and to listen to any objections. The management equivalent to 'a stitch in time saves nine' is 'an explanation at the start saves confusion and delay later on'.

Communication

Communication is successful when it is understood in the fullest sense, that is both in verbal meaning and in intention. Managers cannot become good at it by learning a number of techniques. True, they can improve their communication by clearer thinking and better presentation: knowing what one wants to say, and saying it as simply and clearly as possible, will reduce the risks of misunderstanding. But they are certainly not the whole answer to how to get across what one means. There is even a danger that too much attention to communication, particularly to techniques, may distract attention from the need for cooperation, and without cooperation clear communication is useless.

Good techniques are not enough, because communication, if it is to be successful in getting people both to understand

and to do what is wanted, is a cooperative or two-way process. Its effectiveness depends as much, if not more, on the attitude of the recipient as on the verbal skill of the manager; on the former's ability and willingness to listen as well as on the latter's clarity and sensitivity. It also depends on whether subordinates will say if they have not understood. Communication is, therefore inseparably linked with cooperation. Communication is also a two-way process in a different sense in that managers do not merely give advice and instructions but they also receive advice and information on which to base their decisions. Good upwards communication is as important as good downwards communication. Both can cause difficulties, for what managers say to their subordinates may be misunderstood or misinterpreted, and what they are told may be inadequate or untrue.

Difficulties in downwards communication can arise for a number of reasons. The first need for managers is to realize – and many do not do so sufficiently – that what they are saying is often misunderstood. They must, therefore, be prepared for such misunderstandings and, as far as possible, try to guard against them. The second is to be able to recognize their causes. Verbal misunderstanding, which is the simplest, may be due to a different use of language, especially likely when people have very different backgrounds; to lack of clarity; or to technical jargon. They may also arise from the general tendency to distort, quite involuntarily, any message passed on by word of mouth, which is illustrated in the childish game of repeating a story from person to person. A more difficult barrier to communication is caused by distrust, often leading to a wrong interpretation of what is said and to greater distortion if the message has to be passed on. Where there is an atmosphere of suspicion, even the simplest remark and the most straightforward instruction will be examined for hidden meanings. Managers may find to their astonishment that fantastic interpretations have been put on what they said or, worse, they may go on believing that their subordinates have understood.

The frequency with which management instructions are misinterpreted, and the nature of such misinterpretations, can be a good indication of the level of morale. Perhaps managers should remember, even if they do not feel like acting on it, Dostoevsky's advice in *The Brothers Karamazov*: 'If the people around you are spiteful and callous and will not hear you, fall down before them and beg their forgiveness, for in truth you are to blame for their not wanting to hear you.'[1] Unfortunately for the manager it may be past policies, throwing their shadow forward, which are to blame rather than anything that the present management has done.

Barriers to communication may also be created by a failure to understand that other people have different backgrounds and experience and therefore often do not see and interpret things in the same way. The more widely different the background, the greater the danger of misunderstanding. Yet even people who have similar educational and social backgrounds may make different assumptions, which, if not recognized, can lead to serious misinterpretations. This was illustrated in Tom Burns' study[2] of four men: the manager of a department and the two production engineers and chief designer immediately subordinate to him. It showed that half the time the subordinates thought that their manager had given them information or advice that they could take or not as they thought best, but he thought that he had given an instruction or a decision, which was, therefore, to be obeyed. This was a failure in communication that arose from different assumptions about the role of the manager and the amount of freedom that should be exercised by his subordinates.

Misunderstandings are most likely to arise when there are differences in values. A study by the Acton Society Trust[3] of shop-floor attitudes to promotion showed, for instance, that suspicions of promotion were often due to the different criteria used by management and the shop floor for judging who would make a good foreman. The shop floor gave first importance to being a good craftsman or technician. Management emphasized leadership qualities. Such a difference is

1. Quoted in William H. Whyte, Jr and editors of *Fortune, Is Anybody Listening?*, Simon & Schuster, New York, 1952.

2. 'Directions of Activity and Communications in Departmental Executive Group', *Human Relations*, Vol. VII, No. 1, 1954, p. 95.

3. The Acton Society Trust, *Management Succession*, pp. 74–6, The Trust, London, 1956.

probably irreconcilable, but here, as always, it helps management to understand it and the possible suspicions which may arise in consequence.

Such misunderstandings are likely to be less frequent in manufacturing industry today because of the decline in the proportion of manual workers. The higher proportion of knowledge workers means that there is likely to be less of a gap in values between them and the managers. There are also more opportunities for them to be familiar with the place where they work through lateral job rotation.

Managers need to be sensitive to the areas in which misunderstandings are likely. One of the most usual, and perhaps one of the most neglected, is that of promotion. Many managers seem unaware of the amount of suspicion, speculation, and rumour that so often surrounds promotions. Doubts and suspicions are intensified when manangers are secretive about a new appointment, and then they are surprised if a new manager, whose appointment has caused much speculation and resentment, does not get full cooperation.

There is not only the risk of misunderstanding in upwards communication but also the danger that what managers are told may be incorrect or incomplete; further they may only be told what they have definitely asked about. In the interests of avoiding trouble, or of not worrying him, a manager may receive a simplified, edited, and sometimes wholly untrue version of what is happening. If he does, it will usually be his own fault. He may have made his colleagues afraid to tell him the truth, or anxious not to hurt or worry him. Or he may have asked questions, particularly about their mates or colleagues, which they are unlikely to answer truthfully. Such questions should not be asked. Managers should recognize that people tend to cover up for each other, particularly if they are members of the same social group.

Another barrier to upwards communication can be the manager's unwillingness to listen to employees' problems. Two striking recent examples of this can be cited. In one the girls working in the postroom of a major life assurance company repeatedly reported to the company physiotherapist with back trouble. The physiotherapist looked at the work arrangements and suggested changes that would reduce lifting and stretching, which were two causes of the trouble. The manager refused to consider any changes. In the other example till girls working in a chain store complained of fatigue and asked for shorter shifts. The ergonomist called in recommended stools for sitting at tills and at some counters. The manager rejected the idea, saying 'they are not working unless they are standing up'.

It is not only some British managers who are inadequate in communications. An American survey of 11,000 hourly paid employees in thirty-seven companies between 1978 and 1981 found the greatest dissatisfaction was with communications.[4] In general employees had a favourable view of their supervisors but an unfavourable one of middle and upper management, because they thought corporate communication was bad. Half of those surveyed thought that both upwards and downwards communication was poor and only a third that it was good. But interestingly 83 per cent of them had a favourable view of the personal significance of their work.

One barrier to upwards communication, which is often greater than it need be, is the lack of opportunities, either formal or informal, for employees to say what they are thinking and feeling. Management, when it wishes to explain its views and policies, has notice-boards, house journals, letters, special meetings and a public address system. Workers often have only their union, which may confine itself to wage claims and grievances. Yet both management and workers may prefer to talk about a problem before it reaches the grievance stage. Joint consultation can, if properly used, provide an opportunity to do so. But too often management thinks of it as another means of explaining its policies, rather than as a useful way of finding out what its employees are thinking.[5] The increasing attention being given to methods of promoting worker participation in decision-making may

4. Rabinowitz, William, Falkenbach, Kenneth, Travers, Jeffrey R., Valentine, Glen and Weener, Paul, 'Worker Motivation: Unsolved Problem or Untapped Resource?', *California Management Review*, Vol. XXV, No. 2, January 1983.
5. The use of quality circles is discussed on pp. 49–51.

improve communication. However, one problem is likely to be a gap in communications between workers' representatives on boards or management committees and those they represent.

Despite the limited opportunities for upwards communication between workers and management, they are usually better than the facilities that exist in private industry for junior staff and junior management to tell senior management what they are thinking. Nationalized industries recognized the need for this, and provided consultative and negotiating machinery for all except the most senior levels of management.

Managers, because they tend to underrate the difficulties of communication, usually exaggerate the extent to which it takes place. One illustration of this is the dual assumption made by many managers that their subordinates know what they think of them, and also that they can come and discuss their careers and personal hopes and fears with them when they wish. Yet in practice the day-to-day communications between managers and their subordinates are on immediate work matters, and discussions about a subordinate's progress and career may rarely, if ever, happen informally.

The appraisal and development interview is one example of a formal provision for communication which should, if it is done properly, be a two-way one. Unless these interviews are official policy, few managers will initiate such a discussion with their subordinates, since they may find it embarassing. Still fewer subordinates will do so, even if their manager has an open-door policy. Often the first the manager knows of one of her staff's feelings about her progress is when she comes to say that she is leaving for another job.

So far we have talked about upwards and downwards communication, but much communication also takes place horizontally. It is essential that it should do so, especially when the implementation of a decision affects several departments. Those at the same level should be able to sort out the bugs as they develop and not be prevented by isolation or jealousies from doing so. Top management should, therefore, try to encourage communication between departments at all levels. It can do this partly through the formal organization by the use of interdepartmental committees. It can also try to foster informal contacts by giving managers opportunities to get to know those in other departments. This is one of the values of managers' dining rooms and of company management training courses.

Cooperation

An understanding of what has to be done is necessary for successful implementation. So is a willingness to do it. Implementation may fail because the manager's subordinates or fellow-managers do not cooperate adequately. Again, as in communication, it is helpful to be aware of the possible difficulties in enlisting cooperation. Is there likely to be opposition; if so, from whom and why? Can this opposition be overcome? Is the plan worth the time and effort that may be necessary to do so?

Wise managers know the limits of their authority and, as far as possible, avoid weakening it by trying to exercise it where it is likely to be challenged or ignored. Changes in fashion, for example, may require changes in management's ruling on what is appropriate dress. For female staff more than male staff it would be unwise for management to try to enforce a policy of what is acceptable dress that requires their staff to be unfashionable. Uniforms may be accepted but not restriction on ordinary dress.

Most of what we shall have to say concerns cooperation of workers, but the cooperation of other managers is also vital. Failure to obtain it may have more serious consequences than a failure with one's immediate subordinates. Subordinates who will not cooperate may resign or be moved, but the other managers are likely to remain. Hence 'acceptability to colleagues' is one of the prime criteria for management selection. Yet acceptability alone is sometimes too passive a quality to ensure successful implementation. Persistence, drive, and political manipulation, supported by an understanding of other managers' motives and a correct assessment of the political situation in the organization, may all be necessary to get some plans implemented.

One of the management's main worries, both now and in the past, is how to get the workers' cooperation. A common management pitfall in trying to do so is the desire to find a single solution. Hence the search for panaceas, which for many years has been so marked a feature of management's approach to management – worker cooperation. Each new panacea is seized on enthusiastically by anxious managers. But alack for those who seek an easy solution! Experience and research show that there is no such thing. Any one of the popular answers may be of limited usefulness, given reasonably good morale, but none is the whole or even a major part of the answer and probably all can make a bad atmosphere even worse. Let us look in turn at each of these attempts to promote cooperation and see what lessons can be learnt. The history of each of these panaceas in the UK will be sketched to give a cautionary perspective to current hopes and fashions.

Enlisting Worker Cooperation: the Panaceas

Participation

The advocacy of joint consultation as a way of encouraging better management–worker relations and of increasing productivity has a long history. The first official support for it in Britain came towards the end of the First World War, when the Whitley Committee, in a report approved by the government, recommended that national joint councils should be voluntarily set up in any industry sufficiently organized to make that possible. These councils should, in addition to settling wages and conditions of work, discuss 'the better utilization of the practical knowledge and experience of the workpeople' and 'improvements of processes, machinery and organization, and appropriate questions relating to management and the examination of industrial experiments, with special reference to cooperation in carrying new ideas into effect and full consideration of the workpeople's point of view in relation to them'. This, like some other post-war suggestions for improving management–labour relations, was too much in advance of its time to get much support.[6] Joint consultation was practised in some companies, but the main positive result of this recommendation was the establishment of such committees in government departments, named after the original Whitley Committee, which continue to this day. (These committees are criticized within the Civil Service for their slowness in getting things done, 'waiting for Whitley'.)

The next major attempt to promote joint consultation came from the urgent need in the Second World War for maximum munitions production. Joint Production Consultative and Advisory Committees were set up in many munitions industries. In the words of the engineering agreement, 'The functions of the Committee' were 'to consult and advise on matters relating to productivity and increased efficiency for this purpose, in order that maximum output may be obtained from the factory'. Some of these committees continued after the war. The post-war nationalization Acts provided another boost to the establishment of joint consultative committees. These instructed the Boards to join with the unions to provide for 'the establishment and maintenance of machinery for . . . the discussion of matters affecting the safety, health, and welfare of persons employed . . . and of other matters of mutual interest . . . including efficiency . . .' Each nationalized industry therefore established its own system of consultative committees from local to national level.

During the post-war economic crisis the government again turned to the advocacy of joint consultation as a means of improving productivity. This time the idea was much more enthusiastically received by private industry than it had been after the First World War. Lectures and pamphlets, which may be taken as an index to the amount of interest in a subject, poured forth in the immediate post-war years, extolling and explaining joint consultation.

Yet, as Clegg says in his review of the history and results of joint consultation:

6. For example, the effective opposition of British employers to the industrial charter proposed by those who first set up the Federation of British Industries, which would have guaranteed minimum wages, granted generous redundancy payments, and provided fringe benefits.

. . . Despite the advantage of statutory support in the nationalized industries, government encouragement, and the blessing of
personnel management in private industry, it is much easier to
write off joint consultation's subsequent history as a failure than
to discover its successes.

According to their attitudes, observers expected joint consultation to increase productivity, to raise the standards of labour
relations, or to improve the conditions of the workers – or
perhaps all three. But it is not easy to show that joint consultation has affected any of them, and this is as true of nationalized
industry as of private undertakings.[7]

The reasons Clegg gives for failure are, first, that joint consultative committees and councils are frequently by-passed;
secondly, that there is no difference in principle between this
kind of consultation and collective bargaining (in both, if there
is disagreement, the defeated party may try to bring pressure);
thirdly, and of special importance in the nationalized industries, that the limited authority of local management means
that many queries raised by workers' representatives cannot
be settled at the local level; and, fourthly, that management
has not made joint consultation work. Both the third and the
fourth may cause feelings of frustration among the workers'
representatives. In the nationalized industries a query raised
at local level may have to be referred upwards to the district
and even to the national level. The unwillingness of management to make joint consultation work is likely to be specially
great where managers are forced to set up committees either
because of the nationalization Acts or because, in private
industry, of the enthusiasm of top management, which may
not be shared by middle management.[8]

Two things, according to Clegg, writing in 1960, could be
said with some certainty about joint consultation in private
industry: it had, by and large, done best in progressive and
prosperous firms; and private industry made much less use of
joint consultation in 1960 than it did ten years before. Like
other panaceas, 'It is no longer considered to be the means of

7. Clegg, H. A., *A New Approach to Industrial Democracy*, p. 26, Basil
Blackwell, Oxford, 1960.
8. ibid., pp. 38–41.

establishing a harmonious industrial society. Instead it is given a place as one amongst a number of "tools" of management which may be useful in dealing with some of the awkward social situations with which management may be faced'.[9] It seems clear that joint consultation works best where it is least needed – nor have the studies shown that there is a causal connection between good labour-relations and joint consultation. Perhaps, as Clegg put it, 'A competent management can improve output and labour relations, and, if need be, also make a joint-consultative committee work'.[10]

Joint consultation makes less demands upon management than participation in decision-making. Many European countries have gone much further than the UK towards participation. It seems clear that, whatever new legislation may bring, British managers will have increasingly to learn to live with participation. How successfully they manage to do this will depend, according to Fox,[11] whose thought-provoking book appears in the select bibliography, upon the level of trust created. This in turn, in his view, can only be achieved through greater equality.

Profit-sharing

The supporters of profit-sharing have had even higher hopes of its value than the advocates of joint consultation and participation. (The two are not, of course, mutually exclusive; both may be practised in the same firm.) The most important among the declared objectives of management according to a 1950 review of profit-sharing by the International Labour Organization[12] were:

1. The prevention of strikes and the improvement of the morale of the workers.
2. The provision of an effective incentive to greater efficiency and increased output.

9. ibid., p. 38.
10. ibid., p. 37.
11. Fox, Alan, *Man Mismanagement*, Hutchinson, London, 1974.
12. Narasimhan, P. S., 'Profit-sharing: A Review', *International Labour Review*, pp. 469–99, December 1950.

3. The achievement of a measure of flexibility in the total payroll enabling an automatic adjustment of the total remuneration of labour to business fluctuations.
4. The reduction of labour turnover and stabilization of the labour force.
5. The promotion of thrift and a sense of security among the workers.
6. Greater publicity for the firm.
7. The preservation of capitalism by giving the worker a stake in its continued existence.

In spite of this formidable list of advantages, there has been a high death rate amongst profit-sharing schemes.

The ILO review of profit-sharing concluded that:

> The history of profit-sharing in all countries where it has been left to the voluntary enterprise, as in the United Kingdom and the United States, is full of examples of plans started with high hopes and ended in failure, sometimes after many years of operation.
>
> In a few, rather exceptional cases it has been a spectacular success, but judging from the long list of abandoned plans and the comparatively small number that have endured for more than a few years, the contribution that profit-sharing can make to the promotion of healthy and happy industrial relations and to more efficient production seems to be rather problematical.[13]

The earliest known schemes date back to at least 1820 in France, 1860 in England and 1869 in the USA. In more recent years profit-sharing has been both more and less popular than joint consultation as a means of enlisting the workers' cooperation and promoting a sense of belonging. Quantitatively less popular, a survey of the United States Bureau of Labor Statistics for 1945–6 showed that out of the 15,636 companies covered only about 300 (2 per cent) had profit-sharing plans for their workers. In the UK at the end of 1954 there were, according to the *Ministry of Labour Gazette*,[14]

13. Narasimhan, P. S., op. cit., p. 481.
14. 'Profit-sharing and Co-Partnership Schemes', *Ministry of Labour Gazette*, pp. 165–9, HMSO, London, May 1956.

297 undertakings with profit-sharing schemes applying to all employees; this number did not include those in cooperatives. The British schemes had 321,064 participants.

Interest in profit-sharing and co-ownership schemes has continued, stimulated by employees' increasing demands for greater participation in industry. More positive government encouragement was provided in the UK as a result of the recommendations of the 1978 Finance Act for a clearer tax benefit when a company uses part of its profits to acquire shares for employees through a trust.[15]

A 1978 survey by the British Institute of Management of 622 companies in the UK found that 40 per cent of them had some kind of profit-sharing scheme, but of those 246 companies 71 per cent distributed cash, not equity shares. Less than one quarter of the cash-distributing companies said they would consider handing out shares even if a tax advantage was gained.[16] By 1984, after some changes to the share option scheme in the 1981 Finance Act, there were 7000 schemes with 1.5 million people covered.[17]

Quality Circles

A much more recent panacea is quality circles.[18] They have an appeal because they are an introduction from Japan, and British, and even more American, managers have been keen to try and discover the reasons for the success of Japanese management. Quality circles are the way of giving effect to the Japanese support for bottom-up management. They consist of small groups of between five and ten employees who work together and volunteer to meet regularly to solve job-related problems. The circles are usually, but not always, led by the supervisor and generally meet in company time,

15. Finance Act 1978 (Chapter 42), Part III, Chapter III, HMSO, London, 1978.

16. *Employee Financial Participation*, BIM, London, 1978.

17. *Financial Times*, 1 August 1984. The figure of 700 cannot be compared with the 1978 survey as that was of a limited number of companies.

18. Information about quality circles is taken from Bradley, Keith and Hill, Stephen, 'After Japan: The Quality Circle Transplant and Productive Efficiency', *British Journal of Industrial Relations*, pp. 291–311, November 1983.

weekly or monthly. They aim to improve quality, reduce production costs, raise productivity and improve safety. Participants decide their own topics for discussion. All are trained to use techniques of quality management, including elementary statistics.

Three assumptions underlying quality circles distinguish them from the other panaceas discussed. One, that all employees are capable of improving efficiency and quality. Two, that there is a reservoir of relevant knowledge among employees which is not easily tapped by other methods. Three, that quality is an integral part of production and is the responsibility of every employee.

The quality circle movement has spread round the world. In Japan where it started 4 million employees were estimated to be in circles in 1978. In 1981 there were reported to be circles in 750 US corporations and governmental agencies and in more than 100 British companies. There were also circles in many other countries.

A study by Bradley and Hill of the experience of quality circles in five US and five UK companies, and a more in-depth study of the experience in one British and one American manufacturing company, point to the potential value of quality circles and to their limitations in a different cultural setting.[19] In the two companies quality circles had produced efficiency gains. The authors say:

> Our investigations support the evidence available in published sources, that harnessing employees' accumulated job knowledge shows through in the bottom line, and demonstrates, in addition, that employees themselves believe they have a significant contribution to make.

The authors also found that the circles improved communication between labour and management, but they point to difficulties:

> Line managers suggest by their actions that they do not fully trust quality circles, and attempt to guide the harnessing of

19. Bradley and Hill, op. cit., pp. 307–8.

employee expertise lest it expose managerial inadequacy or organizational ineffectiveness. The fact that some quality circles in these two companies and elsewhere have already withered confirms that successful institutionalization can be difficult to achieve in Western companies.

Quality circles like the other methods discussed are not a panacea for improving management–worker relations. They are one possible method, amongst others, of trying to reduce the level of distrust between labour and management.
As the authors conclude:

> If they are going to be effective and have a long-term future, then the most senior levels of management must be actively involved and demonstrate a continuing commitment to provide the conditions necessary for their success.

Incentive Payment Systems

The advocates of profit-sharing and joint consultation believe that these will stimulate and encourage the workers to take more interest in the company, to identify with it and therefore to wish to increase productivity. A different approach, although, again, not a mutually exclusive one, is the belief that workers will produce more if doing so increases their earnings: hence payment by results, which was for many years, and is still often today, the most popular method for enlisting workers' cooperation in high productivity.

The importance of incentive pay schemes is shown by the high proportion of British companies that have them: three-quarters in 1977.[20] The percentage of employees covered by these schemes has been increasing. Between April 1974 and April 1984 the percentage of all employees who received incentive payments went up from 28.7 to 33.8 per cent, the main increase being for non-manual occupations.[21] Incentive

20. *Incentive Payments Schemes 2*, Income Data Services, Study No. 143, April 1977.
21. New Earnings Survey 1974 and 1984, Part D, Analysis by Occupation. Department of Employment, HMSO, 1974 and 1984.

schemes have a long history; they come in many enthusiastically advocated and vigorously decried types and forms. The
literature on the subject is immense, but much of it is too
partisan to be of use in trying to find out whether and, if
so, in what circumstances and in what form, an incentive
payment system can be of help. However, there is also a
considerable amount of research results.

R. Marriott first reviewed the research and opinion on the
subject in 1957 and published his fourth edition in 1971. He
concludes that:

> Judging by the available evidence of the world-wide use of
> incentive payment systems, their increase in recent years, and the
> greater acceptance of them by trade unions, it seems likely that
> where they can be applied, they will be in most cases. The
> evidence also suggests that among the weekly wage incentive
> systems, the simplest, from the point of view of installation,
> maintenance and worker understanding, is most often chosen.
> This is especially so in the case of piece-work though this may be
> partly a matter of long habit or tradition or the difficulty of
> changing to another system. There is, however, a tendency for
> individual methods to give way to group schemes and for a
> growth in the number of collective schemes whether used alone
> or in conjunction with other financial incentives. These trends
> are a rough indication that under present conditions experience
> has shown all incentive payment schemes to be more advan-
> tageous than otherwise.[22]

He goes on to say that:

> . . . social scientists are agreed that however potentially effective
> a financial incentive may be, it cannot reach its maximum of
> effectiveness and, in fact, will often fail unless installed and
> maintained in the most encouraging circumstances.

One of the Income Data Services[23] provides a useful guide to
some of these circumstances, as follows:

22. Marriott, R., *Incentive Payment Systems: A Review of Research and
Opinion*, 4th edition, p. 94, Staples Press, London, 1971.
23. Income Data Services Study No. 140, *Income Pay Schemes: I*,
February 1977.

The consensus of opinions from the specialists and from our investigations, show that the success of an incentive scheme will hinge on the following factors:

The scheme must be individually tailored to suit the organization involved.

The role and purpose of the scheme for all the participants must be spelt out.

The conditions peculiar to the organization involved, internal and external, will dictate the most appropriate scheme. Failure to recognize these conditions has caused many of the problems in existing schemes. Financial gains alone should not be used to measure the success of a scheme because many intangible benefits cannot be measured in this manner.

Today, incentive schemes are much less often thought of as providing, by themselves, the necessary motivation for workers to reach an optimum level of productivity. Progressive managers now look on them, like the other panaceas, as a possible part of a much wider setting that must include human relations and technical and organizational efficiency.

This setting is all the more important since an incentive can only be effective if it increases workers' willingness to work, as distinct from their capacity to do so, which may be increased through better equipment and organization, or through an improvement in physical or mental health. All schemes for increasing the workers' cooperation are based on the assumption – for which there is plenty of evidence – that there may be a gap, sometimes a large gap, between workers' willingness to work and their capacity to do so. This gap is not, of course, confined to manual workers, as disincentives to effort can, and do, operate at all levels. Let us therefore turn to what is known about workers' motivation and willingness to work.

Motivation

Motivation is a prime task for many managers. Many find it a perplexing one. The best way for a social scientist to become rich is to peddle an answer, particularly a simple answer, to how to motivate employees to work well for the organization. Unfortunately research has shown that there are no simple answers. Motivation is much more complex and varied than the early theories suggested. Later research provides, according to David Guest in a review of research into motivation, little or no support for the previously popular theories of Maslow and Herzberg.[24] But there is evidence from the studies over the years that is useful to managers. First managers need to examine their views about human nature.

The incentives that management provides for its employees will depend, at least to some extent, on its views of why people work and what they want from their work. Douglas McGregor,[25] an American social scientist, produced his now famous distinction between managers who believe in Theory X and those who believe in Theory Y. The former believe that the willingness to work is mainly influenced by external factors, such as an incentive payment scheme, that people are naturally lazy and have to be motivated, pushed, and prodded to work. The latter think that the desire to work is primarily internal, that most people want to do a good day's work but need a favourable environment in which to do it. If management thinks the former is more important, it will seek for ways of devising effective incentives and means of checking that people are working hard. If it believes more in the latter, it will be more concerned with trying to provide a satisfactory working environment in which people are not frustrated and can take an interest in their work. Whichever it believes, most managements now probably accept the fact that workers' attitudes have an effect on productivity, hence the interest in attitude surveys.

Since a large part of the manager's job is getting things done through people, it is essential to try to understand people's motivation. Managers tend to err in one of two

24. Guest, David, 'What's New in Motivation?', *Personnel Management*, pp. 20–3, May 1984.
25. McGregor, Douglas, *The Human Side of Enterprise*, McGraw-Hill, New York, 1960.

directions in their expectations of how their subordinates will
behave. They may expect them to react in the same way
as they themselves would, and think them bloody-minded
if they do not; conversely, they may think of their subordinates as being different human beings, with markedly
different and much simpler motivations, from themselves.
The latter attitude was illustrated in a study of different levels
in industry – workers, foremen and general foremen.[26]
Each was asked what satisfaction they most wanted from
their jobs; the foremen and general foremen were also asked
what they thought their subordinates wanted. The superiors
consistently overrated the importance of economic factors
to their subordinates and underestimated the importance
of social satisfactions, such as 'getting along well with the
people I work with' and 'a good chance to do interesting
work'. The superiors would have been far more accurate
in their estimates of what their subordinates wanted if
they had assumed they wanted much the same as they did.
This is a useful general guide, but managers also need to
recognize that people differ in what they consider important
in a job.

A major study by Blackburn and Mann[27] of 1,000 workers
in jobs requiring relatively low skills provides useful information about what these workers wanted from their work.
The authors found a wide variety of orientations to work.
The phrase 'orientations to work' is used by sociologists to
mean a persisting tendency to seek certain goals and rewards
from work that exists independently of the nature of the
work or its content. Blackburn and Mann found that these
workers' orientations included outdoor or indoor work,
autonomy, working conditions, worthwhileness, work-
mates, pay, hours and promotion. Some individuals had two
main orientations, generally one stronger and one weaker
one.

One of the most useful findings for the manager from

26. Kahn, Robert L., 'Human Relations on the Shop Floor', in *Human
Relations and Modern Management*, edited by E. M. Hugh-Jones, pp. 49–51,
North-Holland Publishing Co., Amsterdam, 1958.

27. Blackburn, R. M. and Mann, M., *The Working Class in the Labour
Market*, Macmillan, 1979.

studies of people's motivations is that, as Blackburn and Mann and other researchers have found, individuals want different things from work. They will, therefore, be satisfied in different jobs and in different organizational cultures – the culture of an organization is shown in the distinctive ways in which employees think and act towards each other, to their customers or clients, and in their attitudes to the organization. Management's task is to try to match what the employee wants from work and what the organization has to offer.

Management's task is also to try to obtain commitment. This idea underlies a bestseller of the early 1980s, *In Search of Excellence* by Peters and Waterman.[28] It was expressed tersely by John Harvey-Jones, chief executive of ICI, Britain's largest chemical company, when he said: 'The real purpose of management is motivation of the group to use its energy to achieve objectives'. The same idea was described more fully by McGregor, writing more than twenty years earlier:

> To create conditions which will generate active and willing collaboration among all members of the organization – conditions which will lead people to *want* to direct efforts towards the objectives of the enterprise . . . *people often expend more energy in attempting to defeat management's objectives than they would in achieving them*. The important question is not how to get people to expend energy, but how to get them to expend it in one direction rather than another. For management, the answer lies in creating such conditions that efforts directed towards the objectives of the enterprise yield genuine satisfaction of important human needs.[29]

Many years later William Ouchi produced his Theory Z in his attempts to see what useful lessons could be learnt for

28. Peters, Thomas J. and Waterman, Robert H., Jr., *In Search of Excellence: Lessons from America's Best-Run Companies*, Harper and Row, New York, 1982.

29. McGregor, Douglas, 'Changing Patterns in Human Relations', *Conference Board Management Record*, Vol. 12, No. 9, p. 366, New York, September 1950.

American business from the Japanese approach to management.[30] He identified their strategies as long-term employment, a specific stated organizational philosophy for each organization commonly emphasizing cooperation and teamwork, and intensive socialization. The last means that, as in the armed services, great attempts are made to teach the new recruits the ways and attitudes of the organization that they have joined. The motivational techniques that Ouchi advises as Theory Z are open communication, consultative decision-making and concern for the employee.

Another useful guide for managers trying to improve motivation comes from what is called 'expectancy theory', which argues that employees perform well when they see a link between effort, performance and rewards, and that an incentive payment scheme may not be seen in this way. David Guest summarized what this theory tells managers that they should do to get a highly motivated workforce. They should:

Systematically identify goals and values within the workforce and survey attitudes and perceptions.

Provide rewards on an individual basis, tied to performance, rather than on a general basis. An overall pay rise, for example, will have little motivational impact.

Make the selective provision of rewards public, so that all employees can see a link between good performance and higher rewards. This will influence expectations.

Make sure subordinates have the knowledge, skills and understanding necessary to their role to translate motivation into high performance.[31]

The current state of research into motivation suggests that if managers want to raise motivation, they need to consider many aspects of their personnel policy. The starting point is the need to recognize that the task is to obtain commitment rather than to exercise control. Next to accept that individuals want different things from work and hence will be

30. Ouchi, William G., *Theory Z: How American Business Can Meet the Japanese Challenge*, Addison-Wesley, Boston, 1981.
31. Guest, David, op. cit., p. 22.

motivated by different rewards, using the word 'reward' broadly to include the wide range of non-financial ones. This means that selection should seek to match what the job offers with what the individual wants. Managers should seek to understand how workers explain what happens and whether they feel that they can control their rewards. Good communication is, therefore, vital. The more that workers see that they can influence rewards, and the rewards that matter to them personally, the more they are likely to be motivated.

No Panaceas, but a Challenge to Management

Our brief survey of the search for panaceas to solve all problems of management–labour cooperation shows that there are none. The belief, for instance, that payment by results is the answer to enlisting workers' cooperation in higher productivity is based on too simple a view of human motivation. Now that so many studies have shown that workers are interested in other things as well as money, that they may place a higher value on social satisfactions – that is, recognition of them as people, and congenial working relationships – than on take-home pay, there is a challenge to management. The challenge is to provide the conditions in which people will want to work and, therefore, to cooperate.

One reason why these panaceas failed to fulfil what was expected of them is that they were so often pursued without the management philosophy that would give them a chance of contributing to better relations. Both participation and profit-sharing imply a particular management–worker relation, stemming from a philosophy of management. Without the right philosophy any scheme for improving management–worker relations is hollow; with it, any scheme can be correctly seen as a possibly useful means for expressing and implementing it, rather than as a cure-all for bad relations. This philosophy must be based on a belief in the dignity and value of each individual in the company – individuals, not hands or numbers. Such a belief will carry with it a recognition that people should be consulted before changes that directly affect them are made.

One problem that worries some top managers is how to

make certain that their junior and middle managers have the same philosophy as themselves. This is particularly likely to be a problem when there is a change in top management, for instance, through nationalization, privatization, or a merger. A new, more progressive top management may find that the middle managers, especially, have quite different ideas of the way employees should be treated. The problem will solve itself eventually as managers retire or leave, but, as Keynes said, 'in the long run we are all dead'. This may be true for a company too.

Since the philosophy of management is vital to the relations between management and its employees, what kind of people are made managers is one of the most important decisions for an organization. To this problem we shall, therefore, turn in the next chapter.

SUMMARY

A manager who is to be successful in getting decisions implemented by other people must organize efficiently, communicate clearly, and secure people's willing cooperation. One danger is that many managers underrate the difficulties of communication, both of conveying to their subordinates what they want done and why, or of getting reliable information from them. Hence, they may be startled when their actions and motives are misinterpreted. Another danger is that managers may fail to realize the need to enlist the cooperation of subordinates. Yet another is that, although aware of the need, they may expect some panacea as the answer to the problems of winning cooperation.

We looked at the history of participation, profit-sharing, incentives and quality circles and saw that there is no evidence that any of them are the magic talisman that so many managers are looking for. At best they may be a useful tool where management–worker relations are already good. So many attempts to improve worker cooperation fail because they are based on the wrong assumptions about motivation and derive from the wrong management philosophy. Research into motivation shows that managers should consider many aspects of their personnel policy if they want to improve motivation. The problems of securing willing cooperation pose a challenge to management: a challenge to provide the conditions in which people will want to work, and, therefore, to cooperate. the prime task is to obtain commitment rather than to exercise control.

4

Leadership and Development

'Leadership' sounds more dynamic than 'management': it has an emotional appeal. The British and Americans are particularly keen on the word – the Americans even more than the British. Hence it is often used in these two countries instead of management, with 'leader' instead of 'manager'. Yet leading is only one aspect of management, an aspect that is more important in some jobs, and at some times, than others. Sometimes it is vital for success, sometimes it is unnecessary. It is more important in times of difficulty and of rapid change than in stable and routine settings. It is important when the manager needs to enlist commitment to a difficult or dangerous task, hence the interest in leadership in the armed services. It is vital when a change of direction is needed and people must change their attitudes and customary ways of working. This was true for many organizations in the 1980s, hence the call for leaders. What 'leaders' meant was managers who had the ability to point the way and to get people committed to going that way. This ability matters most at the top of the organization, particularly of one that needs to change rapidly.

There are many definitions of leadership, as is true of any much studied subject. Common to most of them is the capacity to influence others. The *Penguin English Dictionary*

defined it as 'exercise of authority in a social group'. Other
even simpler definitions are 'to guide' or 'to show the
way'. Academics have produced many more elaborate ones
that seek to explain what is behind leadership: for example,
'interaction between members of a group that initiates and
maintains improved expectations and competence of the
group to solve problems or attain goals'.[1]

The nature of leadership and what makes for effective
leadership have been major subjects for research in the USA
since the late 1940s. So great has been the volume of research
that a large handbook summarizing the results was first published in 1974[2] and a second revised version in 1981.[3]

Much of the research, though called leadership studies,
is equally applicable to understanding management. It is
merely that the word 'leader' has been preferred to manager.
There are, of course, studies, particularly of leadership in
small groups, where the word leader is the correct one. The
first part of this chapter presents the research findings that are
relevant to managers.

Research into Leadership

Leadership Qualities

What are the qualities of a good leader or a good manager?
This question has remained popular over many years. Multi-
tudinous qualities have been said to be not merely desirable
but essential for a good manager. The usual lists of vague,
undefined qualities are no help in management selection and
development. They also call for paragons, whereas all organizations must make do with imperfect human beings.
However, there have been attempts to make more carefully
defined lists based on observation. Two of the more thought-
provoking of these lists are given below. These lists, though
compiled more than twenty years ago, are equally applicable

1. Stogdill, R. M., *Handbook of Leadership: A Survey of Theory and
Research*, Free Press, New York, 1974.
2. ibid.
3. Bass, B. M., *Stogdill's Handbook of Leadership: A Survey of Theory and
Research*, Free Press, New York, 1981.

today. The first is of the characteristics of successful businessmen compiled by Professors Edwards and Townsend, who
said that 'in varying combinations and proportions these
qualities seem to be found in the leadership of most businesses that have grown substantially'.[4]

1. Strength and willingness to work hard, immensely hard in some
   cases.
2. Perseverance and determination amounting at times to fanatical
   single-mindedness.
3. A taste and flair for commerce, an understanding of the market-
   place.
4. Audacity – a willingness to take risks that are sometimes large
   gambles.
5. Ability to inspire enthusiasm in those whose cooperation and
   assistance are essential.
6. Toughness amounting in some men to ruthlessness.

The second list is compiled by Professor Argyris.[5] It is
limited to characteristics that he thinks are helpful in becoming and remaining a successful executive operating in competitive conditions. The characteristics are drawn from
observing numerous American executives, so would not all
be possessed by any one executive. This is in contrast to the
previous list, which was of qualities likely to be found in
most successful businessmen. Argyris's list is:

1. Exhibit a high tolerance of frustration.
2. Encourage full participation and are able to permit people to
   discuss and pull apart their decisions without feeling that their
   personal worth is threatened.
3. Continually question themselves, but without being constantly
   critical of themselves.
   These executives, we would like to emphasize, were keenly
   aware that their personal biases, their personal ways of seeing

4. Edwards, Ronald S. and Townsend, Harry, *Business Enterprise: its growth and organization*, p. 33, Macmillan, London, 1965.
5. Argyris, Chris, *The Personnel Journal*, Vol. 32, No. 2, pp. 50–5, June 1953.

the world, were not necessarily the only or the best ways . . .
They respected their own judgement, not as always being
correct, but as always being made with the best possible intentions. Their self-respect seemed to enable them to respect
others.

4. Understand the 'laws of competitive warfare' and do not feel
   threatened by them.
5. Express hostility tactfully.
6. Accept victory with controlled emotions.
7. Are never shattered by defeat.
8. Understand the necessity for limits and for 'unfavourable decisions'.
9. Identify themselves with groups, thereby gaining a sense of
   security and stability.
10. Set goals realistically.

These two lists portray widely different personalities. In part
this is because the first list was compiled by economists and
the second by a psychologist. It is noteworthy what very
different qualities they select as being important: so much
so, that it is likely that even if they had been looking at the
same people they would still have emphasized different qualities as the reasons for success. The difference between them
highlights the key role company recruiters may play in determining the kinds of personalities who are selected.

The contrast between the two lists is also due to a difference in the kind of successful executive who is being
analysed. The first list seems to be limited to the heads
of companies, the second list seems to include managers at
different levels. (Neither of the authors are very specific on
this point.) The former deals with the entrepreneur, the latter
the professional manager. Both lists could be useful, in
different circumstances, in the examination of promotion
potential, but it would be essential to know what kind of
top manager was needed. Fortunately the best predictor of
success is not the possession of a long list of qualities, but
prior success in similar roles. Hence evidence of leadership at
school and university is a good predictor of future leadership
ability, but that depends upon the situation being compatible
with the individual's personality.

Different Types of Leader

One of the most important findings of the research is that there is not *one* leader's job. This puts the question 'What are the qualities of a good manager?' in a new perspective, since research shows that different situations require different leadership qualities and, therefore, different types of leaders and different kinds of managers. Hence, there is no one type of good manager, nor one set of qualities a good manager will possess. This will be borne out by anyone with wide experience of industry who has noticed the great diversity of character among successful managers. This finding should prompt the managers who are trying to fill a management vacancy to ask 'What is the nature of this particular job?', 'What are its distinctive problems?' and, therefore, 'What kind of manager is needed to fill it?' Unfortunately the answer to these questions cannot be precise because so little is known about which characteristics of a job are important.

Are there some things that all good leaders do? This is one of the questions that interested research workers on leadership. A ten-year inter-disciplinary programme at Ohio State University studied the behaviour of leaders in business, education, the armed services and government. The researchers decided that trying to define the qualities of a good leader was unsatisfactory, and sought instead to define leadership in terms of performance. After a lot of work they finally reduced the basic functions of a good leader to two:

1. *Consideration* or *human relations*, that is, 'the extent to which the executive, while carrying out his leadership functions, is considerate of the staff'.
2. *Initiating structure* or *'get the work out'*, that is, 'the executive organizes and defines the relationship between himself and the members of his staff. He tends to define the role which he expects each member of the staff to assume and endeavours to establish well-defined patterns of organization, channels of communication, and ways of getting jobs done'.[6]

6. Shartle, Carroll, L., *Executive Performance and Leadership*, pp. 120–2, Staples Press, London, 1957.

The original research concerned bomber pilots[7] but the same characteristics exist in industry and in other organizations. Indeed, these two key tasks form the basis for much subsequent research into leadership. They are also used in such training programmes as the Blake and Mouton grid, which rates participants from 1 to 9 on their score for each. Hence a 9/9 manager is the rare person who has the maximum score on each. Good managers should be above average in developing warm relations with their staff and in initiating new ways to solve problems. But the relative importance of the two will vary in different types of work.

There is a conflict between human relations and getting the work out, a conflict known to many managers. Subordinates demand that their managers should be both powerful and popular, that they should both initiate ideas and move their group towards the goal on the one hand and be considerate on the other.[8] The conflict may be resolved by sharing the roles between two leaders, so that one leader is powerful – gets things done – and the other is popular and looks after the social and emotional needs of the members. One often sees this sharing of leadership qualities, particularly at the top of an organization. It is helpful for managers to be aware of the existence of this conflict and, therefore, of the nature of the choice before them. It may also help them in the selection of a deputy. A manager who is weak on one of the two should probably choose a deputy who is strong there. Managers who are unaware of this conflict may fluctuate in their attempts to satisfy first one demand and then the other, whereas what matters is that both demands are being satisfied within the group, not that the manager must be good at both.

Despite all the evidence of American research in leadership and the popularity of the Blake and Mouton grid, it is possible that a different approach works. This is suggested by a study of Japanese managers in manufacturing companies

7. Halpin, Andrew W., 'The Leadership Behaviour and Combat Performance of Airplane Commanders', *Journal of Abnormal and Social Psychology*, Vol. XLIX, No. 1, pp. 19–22, January 1954.

8. Shartle, op. cit., p. 125.

in this country, which is reported on p. 136. The Japanese managers, the researchers reported, were liked by the workers even though they had a strong task-centred approach.

There are also conflicts between what superiors and subordinates want of the manager. It is difficult for a manager to fulfil the expectations of both and be liked by both. Subordinates are likely to want supervisors who are considerate, while superiors want managers to be primarily concerned with achieving the goals of the organization. This conflict is greatest at the foreman level, since the foreman may be the buffer between the conflicting aims of management and workers.

A key finding of the leadership studies is that leadership in a group may not be concentrated in one person but spread among several. This is illustrated by the previously mentioned two people between them meeting the needs for consideration and for getting the work out. Groups may have other needs, too, if they are to work effectively. Some need a person who comes up with new ideas, who can challenge the sloppy and conforming thinking of other members of the group. Observers of group discussions may notice that contribution. Leadership, in terms of the ability to influence others, is not necessarily identical with formal status. We all know that the amount of influence that a person exerts is a combination of position and personality.

Those responsible for selecting a new manager need to consider not merely the individual's strengths and weaknesses but also those of their future colleagues. This raises most problems when a new managing director is being appointed. Does top management need a thorough shake-up? Unless it does, will the existing people be able to adjust to the new manager's leadership pattern? If not, will their resignations or difficulties hurt the company? The tendency of newly appointed leaders to replace some of their subordinates may be explained by the need to find people who complement them. Managers should also know their own weaknesses and seek to make up for them in the selection of their staff. In this sense there may be some truth in the dictum that 'a good manager can manage anything', because managers who know their own deficiencies in knowledge and personality can try to build up a team to complement them.

One of the questions asked by the research workers on leadership is 'What are the effects of different methods of leadership? Much of the research has tried to compare the effects of a democratic leader – that is, one who encourages participation – with those of an authoritarian leader. Most of it points towards the desirability of the democratic type of leader who encourages participation, places employee welfare before production, but does not give the former undue emphasis, and exercises only a general rather than a close supervision. However, a supervisor can be too employee-centred and this may lead to low production and low morale. Democratic leadership encourages long-term employee development and commitment. Not all employees like a democratic manager; those who have authoritarian personalities prefer an authoritarian boss. Worst of all is *laissez-faire* leadership, which has a bad effect on productivity, cohesiveness and satisfaction.

Managers who are trying to decide what is the best way for them to manage will find that there is no single answer. Useful advice is given in 'How to Choose a Leadership pattern' by Robert Tannenbaum and Warren H. Schmidt.[9] They suggest that there are three factors managers should take into account: their own characteristics, those of their subordinates, and those of the situation.

Managers' characteristics that are important in deciding how to manage are:

1. Their value system, including their views on whether individuals should have a say in decisions affecting them; the importance they attach to efficiency; the personal growth of their subordinates and company profits.
2. Their confidence in their subordinates.
3. Their own leadership inclinations, whether they are more comfortable being a member of a team or being highly directive.
4. Their feelings of security in an uncertain situation, hence their ability to delegate without feeling too worried about the

9. *Harvard Business Review*, Vol. 36, No. 2, pp. 95–101, March–April 1958. This classic article is reprinted in different collections of readings, including Koontz, Harold and O'Donnell, Cyril, *Management: A Book of Readings*, 4th edition, McGraw-Hill, New York, 1976.

resulting uncertainty of the outcome. 'This "tolerance for ambiguity" is being viewed increasingly by psychologists as a key variable in a person's manner of dealing with problems.'

The characteristics of the subordinates that are important are:

1. The strength of their need for independence.
2. Their readiness to assume responsibility for decision-making.
3. Their tolerance for ambiguity; some subordinates have a preference for clear-cut directives, others prefer more freedom.
4. Their interest in the problem and their views on its importance.
5. Their degree of understanding of, and identification with, the goals of the organization.
6. Their knowledge and experience.
7. Whether they have learned to expect a share in decision-making.

The amount of freedom that managers can allow their subordinates will depend upon the extent to which there is a positive answer to the above points.

The characteristics of the situation that are important are:

1. The type of organization, including: the kind of behaviour that is customary, and the limitations placed on employee participation by the size of the establishment, the geographical distribution and the degree of organizational security that is necessary.
2. Group effectiveness; this is important when the delegation is to the group, rather than to an individual.
3. The nature of the problem: for instance, if managers have most of the information that is relevant, it may be easier for them to think it through rather than to brief one or more of their staff.
4. The amount of time available to make a decision will affect the extent to which managers feel they can involve their subordinates in decision-making.

Tannenbaum and Schmidt conclude that successful leaders are those who are both keenly aware of the factors that are relevant to their behaviour at a particular time, and who are also able to act appropriately. They are both perceptive and flexible. This means that when the situation calls for it they will be strong leaders and in different circumstances they will be permissive ones.

Developing Managers

Top managers of progressive companies worry more – or at least more vocally – about how to ensure a supply of good managers than about many other business problems. Millions of words have been written about the question, and fat fees are charged for attempting to educate managers. But what do we really know about it?

Some, although a decreasing number of, managers believe that good managers are born and that little or nothing needs to, or can, be done to help their development, since this will be a natural process of a potentially good manager learning by experience and example. 'You cannot keep a good man down' is their motto, allied to the belief that he will learn for himself, whatever the circumstances. Managers who believe this are obviously not concerned with the problems of how to develop their subordinates. But the number who hold this comforting belief is steadily decreasing. The others are often worried men or women conscious of the increased demand made on management by the rapid changes affecting many organizations. They look anxiously round for those who have the potential to meet these demands. Once found, how are they to be given the necessary training and experience? A still more worrying problem is defining *necessary*.

There would probably be considerable support for a general statement such as the following: 'Managers should first have a knowledge of a specific function, including both theoretical training and experience on the job. Next they must understand management tools, such as budgetary control, standard costs, and increasingly developments in information technology.' A professional background and a grasp of the tools of management are the easy part of the answer to the question 'What training and experience is necessary for a good manager?' Difficulties arise when we think of the core of the manager's job – managing people and making decisions – and consider how to improve performance on both.

A distinction is frequently made between training to improve managers' performance in their present job and education for promotion. This distinction is abhorred by Peter

Drucker, who argues that all training should be for development to meet tomorrow's demands, and that the concept of an elite with high potential is a fallacy.[10] We cannot, he argues, predict a manager's development more than a short time ahead, and we have no right to dispose of people's careers on probability. This is an admirable warning, but large firms may have to judge that one manager is more likely to reach the top than another if they are to give their future top managers sufficient experience on the way up. Some distinctions on promotability are probably necessary, but they can be made without creating a permanent elite.

Those who do distinguish between training to improve performance and education for promotion think of the former as being concerned with technical knowledge and the skills and tools of management, including the ability to write and speak clearly and effectively. Training may also include an attempt to change attitudes to management. Education for promotion is described as 'broadening' – the subject of an immense amount of discussion.

Broadening, whether thought of solely in relation to promotion or as something that should be the aim of all management education, means a deepening of understanding rather than an increase in the amount of knowledge. Such an understanding should cover three areas. First, the manager must understand the nature of the external environment and its effects on the company, which can range from government regulations and the character of the trade unions in the industry, to the general economic situation and the market conditions affecting the firm. In a company with overseas interests, managers may also need to understand something of the economic and social facts in the relevant countries as well as their differences in outlook. Secondly, they must learn to see the business as a whole and the role and problems of each department. Thirdly, their understanding of people's reaction must be deepened, as well as being extended, to include different types of people from those they may have dealt with on the shop floor or in the offices. They will have to learn how to manage managers – both those who work for

10. *The Practice of Management*, op. cit., pp. 159–61.

them and, using the word 'manage' in a different sense, their peers who may be competing with them for promotion, for status, and for scarce resources. Broadening should make managers more aware of all the factors that influence their job and company, more aware of their own reactions and more perceptive of other people's, and more flexible in their approach. It is one thing to describe in very general terms what is meant by broadening, and another to know how to achieve it, or to know whether there is any good general prescription or only individual ones.

One method used, although not so frequently as it is advocated, is job rotation. Those who favour it argue that it widens managers' experience and should make them more flexible. Some also believe that, if managers are to get the necessary experience for top management, their experience must be planned and accelerated, and that if they are to get quickly enough up the management ladder, they must be singled out for such planned experience. Some companies try to ensure that managers get a variety of different types of job by moving them from one department to another, by sending them to foreign subsidiaries or by putting them in a job that gives them a general view of many aspects of the business. The use of this form of development is restricted by the price which may have to be paid in temporary dislocation when a person with no knowledge of a department is put into a vacant post in preference to a suitable person already in that department. The companies using job rotation as a conscious policy are likely to have a general policy of moving people in their early years, and later to practice selective job rotation. Some of the very large companies occasionally create vacancies in order to develop those earmarked for top management. For others with potential, suitable vacancies will be used when they arise. Job rotation as a means of developing managers by widening their experience is fairly straightforward, although there is much we do not know about the mechanics: how long should be spent in the different jobs and what kind of transfers between departments are desirable and practicable?

The area of uncertainty becomes much greater – although some people think they know the answer without offering any evidence of its validity – when we turn to management development by formal education. There are two main queries. What do managers need to know? What should be their attitude to managing, and if they do not have the right attitudes, how can education help to change them? These questions concern the aims of management education. They are fundamental. There are also important queries about methods. On the first question, what a manager should know, there is plenty of scope for disagreement on detail, but there is some agreement on the broad outline, which we discussed earlier in this chapter. The research on leadership can help us to answer the first part of the second question, that is, 'What should be the manager's approach to managing?' The main problem of management development lies in the second part: can we change attitudes, and, if so, how? Many companies, for instance, are worried about how to develop an understanding of, and sensitivity to, people: for instance, how to change good scientists or technicians who have been primarily concerned with things into managers who are sufficiently interested in and aware of people to be sensitive to their reactions, and to be able to adjust their behaviour accordingly.

There is little evidence about the effects of management education on attitudes. Much of the research on effectiveness of management education is inconclusive, partly because of the great difficulty of finding ways of assessing it. However, several studies of the effects of human relations courses for supervisors show that the behaviour of the foreman's boss is very important. If the boss is considerate, this has much more effect on the foreman's behaviour than training courses in human relations.

We do know that attitudes can be changed by drastic means, such as the brain-washing of prisoners or the methods used to change the attitudes of a man or woman entering a monastery or a convent. In a most interesting article, 'Management Development as a Process of Influence', Professor Schein uses these extreme examples to illustrate the process of changing attitudes.[11] This process,

11. Schein, Edgar H., *Industrial Management Review*, Vol. II, No. 11, May 1961.

he says, has three phases. First, unfreezing of present attitudes so that the individual is ready to change. This can be accomplished either by increasing the pressure to change or by reducing some of the threats or resistance to change. Secondly, the actual change of attitude; the person learns new attitudes either by identifying with and emulating some person holding these attitudes, or by being placed in a situation where new attitudes are demanded as a way of solving unavoidable problems. Thirdly, refreezing, that is, the new attitudes become part of the personality.

Professor Schein thinks that unfreezing, or willingness to change one's attitudes, is not likely to be achieved in appraisal interviews or by management training conducted at the place of work, because both these are too related to the manager's normal routine. He thinks that management courses in residential centres, where the manager is isolated from the pressures of daily life, are more likely to provide the setting in which a manager may become willing, and able, to change. Much will depend on the atmosphere of the course and the support it gives to efforts at self-examination. The possibility of any change lasting will depend upon the situation to which managers return. If they go to a different job, or if several of their fellow managers go on a similar course, there is more chance of it doing so. Job rotation can help to unfreeze attitudes and thus make a change of attitudes easier. A move from one setting to another removes many of the supports of the old attitude, thus giving the manager an opportunity to try new ways of behaving and to be exposed to different attitudes.

Professor Schein suggests that a course just before a manager goes to a new job might provide the greatest opportunity for learning and modifying attitudes and behaviour. A post as personal assistant, where a good relationship develops, will influence younger managers to adopt the attitudes of the older, but they will not learn new methods of looking at management problems. Hence, if a broad view is required, job rotation can expose the young manager to a variety of points of view.

The uncertainties about the aims and methods of management education are, or should be, increased by the fact that management consists of so many different jobs and that it is demonstrably possible to manage successfully in many different ways. The very diversity of successful managers must make one pause before offering a general prescription for either what are successful managers or how they should be developed. The research on leadership indicates that one can say, in very general terms, that a good manager is perceptive and flexible and that therefore experience and formal education should be planned to try and develop these qualities.

The move, in some management education, to a more individual approach recognizes the limitations of general lectures to groups of managers, who will differ both in the nature of their jobs and in their styles of learning. A greater emphasis upon the individual's setting and needs can cater for these differences. The growing interest in promoting self-development encourages individuals to adapt what management writers and teachers have to say to their own needs.

How Important is a Good Manager?

We have talked so far as if producing good managers is of key importance to the success of a company. In doing so we have mirrored the views of many top managers today. Yet there is a danger that enthusiasm for management selection and development may place too much emphasis on the manager and too little on the organization. We may be trying to find a cure for the failings of management through management education, when our attention ought first to be directed to the organization in which the manager has to work. How managers manage is only partly due to the kind of people they are, for their behaviour is also affected by the position in which they are placed.

Although we must continue to do all we can to improve the selection and training of managers, we should not think of good managers as the sole, or even necessarily the most important factor in successful management. The culture of the organization, that is, the ways that people customarily behave towards each other, is important in determining how well the organization works. This was more widely recognized by managers in the seventies and eighties than in the fifties or even sixties. This has led to a decreased emphasis upon the importance of leadership and a greater concern for trying to improve the culture of the organization.

SUMMARY

'Leader' is often used instead of 'manager' because it has more appeal. Much of the research into leadership is relevant to managers because leading is one aspect of managing.

The early research into leadership explored three problems: the qualities of leaders, their tasks and what style produces the best performance. The findings show that leadership is more complex and varied than had been expected. There is no one good leader, no one style that works best in all situations, not even just one leader in many groups, for different people may lead in different ways and at different times. However, there is agreement about the tasks, but at such a general level of description – consideration and getting the work out – that its utility is limited. A good leader should be above average on both, although their relative importance will vary with the kind of job to be done.

The traits and abilities needed to lead people tend to vary from one situation to another. This is the reason why selection of managers is so difficult. There needs to be a match between the manager, the subordinates and the situation. Democratic leadership is generally more satisfying and effective than autocratic leadership. But there are exceptions. Bass in his summing up of more than thirty years' research into leadership reminds us that: 'The real test of leadership lies not in the personality or behavior of the leaders, but in the performance of the groups they lead.'[12] By their fruits you shall know them.

Management education can be divided into the acquisition of specific information and skills and the deepening of understanding. The latter covers three areas: one, an awareness of the external environment of the organization and its effects

12. Bass, op. cit., p. 598.

upon it; two, an understanding of the organization as a whole and of the interrelationships of departments; and, three, a greater insight into people's reactions.

Two anxieties were expressed about management education. One was that too little attention is paid in many programmes to the diversity both of jobs and of individual needs and learning styles. Happily, there is some move away from lectures to large groups of managers to a more individual approach that aims to encourage self-development. The other anxiety is that management education may be seen as a cure for problems that have their causes in bad organization and a poor working climate. Good managers are not the only factor in successful management.

Part II

The Organization

The first two chapters describe the organization within which the manager will have to work. The third looks at the relation between the organization and the people who make it work: how they modify the formal organization as well as how the organization affects the ways in which they think and act. For those who are uninterested in problems of organization, the first two chapters may be heavy going. They are advised to read the summaries first and then to decide whether the content is of interest to them.

5

The Setting for Modern Management

Management used to be an easier, more intuitive job than it is today. The vast majority of firms had simple organizations with few managers. Of course, there was specialization, but the division between jobs was often fluid, and the jobs were tailor-made to the individuals available. The sales manager might advise on office management and the works manager might help with the accounts. Relations within management were often informal, so that the foreman could go direct to the managing director with a problem. Rules were few. Decisions were made by hunch based on experience.

Today, the same firm, if it has done even moderately well, will be larger and its organization more complex. The number of managers and specialists will have increased at a faster rate than the number of other employees, thus contributing to the growth in administrative overheads. The management levels will be more numerous and more clearly defined. Specialization of jobs will have increased; the duties of the job may be described in detail together with the qualifications of the person who would be suitable to fill it. Individuals will be fitted to jobs rather than vice versa. Rules will have developed to cover many aspects of the business, such as who is authorized to spend money, how much and on what, or what provision is made when an employee is sick. These rules will apply to categories of people, such as factory managers or manual workers; their application to individuals will depend upon which category they are in.

This brief account of a fair-sized company today could also be used to describe the organization of a hospital, the army or the civil service. It is the description of a bureaucracy. This word is not used disparagingly but with the technical meaning given to it by sociologists for a method of organization that has certain characteristics. These are not only widespread today but also appeared in some earlier civilizations – for instance, in the civil service of ancient China.

Bureaucracy makes possible a rational approach to administration. Hence it develops in any large organization that aims at efficiency and continuity. It may seem strange to say that the reason for the development of bureaucracy is its efficiency, when the word 'bureaucratic' is often used as a synonym for inefficiency; but this refers to possible developments within a bureaucracy and not to its basic characteristics. To these we shall now turn because they can help us to understand the setting within which managers work in any large organization, though some large organizations are more bureaucratic than others. First, we shall give a brief description of these characteristics. Then we shall look at their practical implications for management.

Characteristics of Bureaucracy

There are four main ones. The first is *specialization*. This exists among any group of people working together, but it is highly developed in a bureaucracy. The distinctive feature of specialization in a bureaucracy is that it applies to the job rather than to the individual, so that the job usually continues in existence when the present holder leaves. This makes for continuity. The functions of the job are defined; therefore, the qualifications of the individual who could fill it are, to some extent, specified. The jobholder must have the experience and education required for that post.

The second common feature of all bureaucracies is the

hierarchy of authority, which makes a sharp distinction between the administrators and the administered. In industry it is between management and workers, in the armed services between the officers and the rank and file. Within the ranks of administrators there are also clearly defined levels of authority. This detailed and precise stratification is very marked in the armed forces and the civil service. It exists in many large companies, where both the levels of authority and the rewards at each level are laid down.

The third characteristic of bureaucracy, the *system of rules*, is closely related to the fourth, *impersonality*, since the aim of the rules is an efficient and impersonal operation. The rules are more or less stable, although, of course, some of them will be changed or modified with time. They can be learned, and knowledge of them is one of the requisites of holding a job in a bureaucracy. The existence of these rules is in marked contrast to more informal organizations.

Impersonality is the characteristic distinguishing bureaucracy most clearly from other types of organization: for example, from that based on kinship, which is found in primitive societies and to a lesser extent in civilized societies in, say, some family firms. The allocation of privileges is impersonal in a bureaucracy, as is the exercise of authority, which should be in accordance with the rules laid down and not arbitrary. Hence, in the more highly developed bureaucracies there tend to be carefully defined procedures for appealing against certain types of decisions – the bureaucracy must not only be impersonal but must be seen to be impersonal.

It is the demand for impersonality, the operation of the rules without ill-will and without favour, which makes the acceptance of bribes a cardinal sin for the Western bureaucrat. It is also the reason why unscheduled privilege is viewed with such disfavour and why rules to try to prevent privilege based on favouritism are so carefully developed. This does not, of course, mean that there are no privileges for officials in a bureaucracy, but what there are must be allocated according to definite rules based on rank or seniority. The transition, from the personal bestowal of privileges at the discretion of senior managers to their allocation according to rules, can be seen in many businesses. Nor is it often an easy one. The exact definition of the levels entitled to certain privileges, such as the use of the executive dining-room, can cause many heartaches among those seeking for the privilege, and headaches among the personnel officers trying to define unquestionable rules for its allocation.

These four characteristics of a bureaucracy, *specialization, an hierarchy of authority, a system of rules* and *impersonality*, have developed because they are the most efficient method yet discovered of running a large and continuing organization. They make for efficiency partly because they ensure the continuity essential for any organization that is to last longer than the life of its founder; and partly because they provide, as far as possible, for administration to be carried out on a rational basis by the development of a logical system of rules, of division of work, of qualifications for office, and of defined levels of authority. The scope for human whims is reduced to a minimum.

Reasons for the Growth of Bureaucracy

Increasing Size

This is the most important reason. We saw at the start of this chapter that as a firm grows, specialization increases, there are more levels of authority, and the need for rules to ensure consistency becomes greater. Size also makes orderly administration essential. Smaller companies may still be run successfully just on intuition and drive; in a large company the resulting chaos will be too inefficient.

People often refer to the great predominance of small firms in the British economy. It is true that most firms are small ones, but they employ many fewer people than do large companies, and earn a small proportion of total profits. Relatively speaking, there are very few large companies but they form an important part of the British economy.

Size can be measured in several ways: the number of people employed or the amount of capital invested are the most usual. These measures are often similar, except in companies that need a great deal of capital but have relatively few employees, such as oil refining or cement manufacture.

In the 1930s nearly 40 per cent of all manufacturing employment came from companies employing 200 or fewer employees; by 1973 the proportion had fallen to just under 20 per cent, although it had risen to 22.5 per cent by 1977.[1] This compares with the larger numbers working for manufacturing companies employing 10,000 and over, which show an increase although the figures are for a shorter period.[2] (See Table 5.1.)

TABLE 5.1

	Number of firms employing 10,000 and over	Proportion of total manufacturing employees
1958	74	24.8
1978	83	34.6

During the sixties and early seventies the trend towards acquisitions and mergers and consequently larger size intensified as a result of increased competition and government encouragement. Since 1972 the trend has been considerably less marked.[3] In 1970–1 there were 153 companies employing more than 10,000 people and in 1984–5 there were 155.[4] This small increase camouflages two opposing factors: one, continued growth, particularly by acquisitions, increasing the size of large companies, and, two, the

1. Macey, R. D., *Job Generation in British Manufacturing Industry*, Government Economic Service Working Paper No. 55, Department of Industry, 1982.

2. Business Monitor PA 1002: Report on the Census of Production: summary tables, Business Statistics Office, HMSO, 1981, Table 12.

3. 'Acquisitions and Mergers of Industrial and Commercial Companies; Third Quarter, 1978', *Business Monitor*, p. 1, Business Statistics Office, HMSO, November 1978.

4. *Times '1000' Leading Companies in Britain*, 1970–1 and 1984–5.

reduction in numbers employed during the recession at the
end of the 1970s and early 1980s. The decline was primarily
in the manufacturing companies, where the numbers
employing 10,000 and over went down from 83 in 1978 to
66 in 1981.[5]

Manufacturing companies are only one form of large-scale
organization; there is also commerce, the nationalized industries, the civil service, the National Health Service, the armed
services, and much of local government. Between them these
employed in 1976 approximately 6.7 millions, which,
together with those employed by the top 100 industrial companies, meant that in 1977 some 10.4 millions or 42 per cent
of the total employed population worked for large-scale
organizations.[6] All of these had at least some of the characteristics of a bureaucracy.

Greater Complexity

This is partly a by-product and partly a cause of increasing size. It makes a rational, highly specialized organization
imperative. Two important contributors to greater complexity
are the growth of government regulations and increasing
mechanization. The latter also makes for stricter discipline.
What has to be done is laid down rather than left to a
craftsman's judgement.

Scientific Management Movement

The advocates of scientific management stress rational,
prescribed procedures. Hence many of the management consultants are trying to promote bureaucracy – although, if
they only thought of the word in its popular sense, they
would be horrified to be told so! They advise a carefully
planned organization, with clearly defined levels of authority, and specialized jobs that are described in detail.

5. Business Statistics Office, HMSO, 1981, Table 12.
6. Figures calculated from those provided in *Annual Abstract of Statistics
1977*, Chapter IV, 'Labour Statistics', pp. 151–71, HMSO, 1977.

Demands for Equality of Treatment

This is a different type of reason for the growth of bureaucracy, one which is influenced by the ideology prevailing at that time and place. It can be, and in Britain is, an important factor in increasing bureaucracy. Citizens want equality of treatment from the civil service, and questions in the House try to ensure that they get it, thereby putting pressure on civil servants to administer strictly in accordance with the rules, so that no questions will be asked. Employees, through their union, strive for the acceptance of rules to ensure that management cannot discriminate between individuals at its own discretion.

One of the trade unions' reasons for favouring nationalization was that it would give them greater power to enforce their demands for fairness. The history of the nationalized industries shows the way in which such demands can lead to increasing bureaucracy. Fairness is usually identified with equality of treatment. Hence variations in the conditions of work within one large organization are likely to be challenged as unfair. If rules and procedures that are demonstrably fair by this standard are to be devised, little or no allowance can be made for local difficulties and preferences.

The power of those who complain of inequality of treatment to bring pressure upon senior officials is important in determining the extent to which rules are made to ensure impersonal treatment. Civil service rules are the most carefully devised. The nationalized industries, which legally have to consult with their employees on matters directly affecting them, were committed to developing a more carefully defined personnel policy than private industry. Later legislation extended the demands for equality to private industry. The client and the employee when they are organized to demand equality of treatment both exert pressure towards greater bureaucracy. Yet, being human and therefore paradoxical, they may complain of bureaucracy when these rules are applied to themselves, and condemn an unfeeling machine that takes no account of individuals.

Limitations on the Growth of Bureaucracy

Why with such powerful forces pressing towards greater bureaucracy is there not even more of it in business today? There are great differences in the extent to which bureaucracy has developed, not merely between the large firm and the medium-size one but between firms of the same size. What are the reasons for these variations and what factors make for more or less bureaucracy? But first what is a more developed bureaucracy? It is popularly equated with the amount of red-tape, yet this, although it may be a by-product, is not a criterion by which one can judge the amount of bureaucracy; one may merely be judging the efficiency of the O and M department! Rather the criterion is the extent to which the four characteristics of bureaucracy have developed.

There are two main limitations on the growth of bureaucracy. The first is management attitudes and philosophy and the second the pressure of rapid change.

Management Attitudes and Philosophy

We have seen powerful reasons why managers of large companies should make them more bureaucratic. The extent to which they do so will depend partly on their attitude to management and the kind of people they are and partly on the situation of their companies. Some managers dislike the orderly administration characteristic of a bureaucracy. They may find it irksome, even unbearably so, to be bound by the rules. They may attach great value to intuition and initiative. They may prefer to reward where they think fit, paying the salary that they think the individual is worth and giving the privileges that they think are deserved. They may trust their own judgement in selection and expect individuals to mould the jobs to suit themselves, rather than choose a person to fit a job specification. In sum, they may believe that initiative is only fostered in a free-wheeling company, where people are able to enlarge their jobs and to earn as much as they prove themselves to be worth.

The attitudes and personality of top management will,

therefore, influence the amount of bureaucracy in the company. But even if management is opposed to bureaucracy, there are, as we have seen, powerful pressures towards it, which makes it difficult for a large company to prosper without a bureaucratic framework.

The prevailing management philosophy will influence management actions. Earlier the emphasis was on the technical advantages to be derived from size and from making use of the most qualified expert. Now there is greater concern for human reactions, for choosing the right people and giving them more freedom to manage.

Pressure of Change

An organization in a rapidly changing situation cannot, if it is to be successful, be very bureaucratic; jobs change, authority relationships become more flexible and many of the rules cease to be appropriate. Therefore, the situation in which the organization operates will influence the amount of bureaucracy that is possible. The rapid change that has affected many organizations in recent years has necessarily led to a decline in the amount of bureaucracy. So has the move to create smaller semi-autonomous units within larger organizations.

Managers in a Bureaucracy

What are the implications for junior and middle managers of working in a large organization today? It will have both advantages and disadvantages for them, and fewer advantages for the managers who prefer to do their own thing. Managers will be appointed for their qualifications rather than for their connections. The greater the belief in the need for qualifications, the smaller becomes the personal element in appointment. This will suit young managers who are looking for a post and are short of connections. They may be less enthusiastic when they want to appoint new staff and find that their freedom is restricted by the appointments procedure.

Managers in a bureaucracy are expected to be loyal to the

organization rather than to a person. In return the organization looks after them as long as they fulfil their duties. What is meant by 'fulfilling one's duties' varies considerably, but in some British businesses security of tenure for managers used to be nearly as great as for the established civil servant. The recession of the late seventies and early eighties changed that for many managers, particularly in manufacturing companies.

The bureaucracy also offers its officials an established pattern of career expectations. Many businesses are still less bureaucratic in this respect than the civil service and the armed forces. But there is pressure from the young graduates coming into industry for more information about their job and salary expectations. So far this pressure has been only partly successful; young managers may still be told 'it is up to you'.

One of the great advantages for managers of working in a bureaucracy is that they are free from much former arbitrariness. They will know much better where they stand in the organization. Their responsibilities and authority will be laid down. Good work will be more likely to be rewarded by promotion, since bureaucracies try to make an impersonal assessment of merit. Privileges and, to some extent, pay will be determined by the post occupied rather than by their standing with their bosses. However, the flexibility and secrecy of salaries which still exists in some companies is another of the ways in which they are unbureaucratic.

In a bureaucracy greater emphasis is placed on the value of professional skill, on a rational, matter-of-factness. This means that managers must be able to convince others of the correctness of their judgement. However, being human, their willingness to be convinced will depend partly on whether they get on well with them.

One of the disadvantages for managers of working in a bureaucracy is that their freedom of action will be curtailed. They will be restricted by the definition of their job's responsibilities and authority. They are the occupant of a continuing post that has certain duties and privileges attached to it. They must manage within the rules of the organization and accept the limitations on their authority, including their authority over their staff. Some managers will consider these disadvantages a small price to pay for greater security and steady advancement by merit; others may reluctantly adjust to this form of management or devote part of their energy to finding ways of evading the rules and increasing their freedom of action. Yet others will choose to work in a less bureaucratic, more free-wheeling, company where their chances of rapid promotion may be greater.

The Problems of Bureaucracy

The problems of bureaucracy are the problems of balance. The characteristics of bureaucracy: specialization, a hierarchy of authority, a system of rules and impersonality, help to make for efficient and continuing organizations but only if they are not developed to excess.[7] There are two main dangers: one, that what should only be means become ends in themselves; two, that insufficient allowance is made for different or for changing conditions.

The classic danger in a bureaucracy is of course an over-emphasis on rules; hence the stereotype of a bureaucrat as a man who punctiliously keeps to formal procedures however inappropriate – the man who hoists the flag while the building is burning. The existence of rules inevitably limits flexibility. One reason why 'bureaucratic' is often a slur word is because a bureaucracy is necessarily impersonal in the administration of its rules and is often accused of inhumanity. Hence one of the problems of a bureaucracy is how to combine the development of impersonal rules that prevent favouritism with sufficient flexibility to deal with the hard case that does not fit the rules. Impersonality can be modified by the way in which the rules are devised, so that some latitude is left to the managers in interpreting them to meet a hard case. Bureaucracies must be impersonal, but the individuals in them can

7. Readers who are interested in a discussion on the 'pathologies of bureaucracy', particularly red-tape or empire-building, are referred to March, I. G., and Simon, H. A., *Organizations*, pp. 36–47, Wiley, New York, 1958; and Parkinson, C. Northcote, *Parkinson's Laws and other Studies in Administration*, Houghton Mifflin, Boston, 1957.

strive to be humane in their interpetation of the rules and in the way they behave to others.

Another obvious danger of bureaucracy is rigidity: hence an inability to adapt fast enough to changing conditions. This is most likely in a company where the managers are used to stable conditions and now find that their old methods are unsuited to a changing market.

Yet another potential weakness of bureaucracy is the development of the 'organization' man.[8] Any organization must try to ensure that its members further its objectives, and will seek to do so by the use of discipline, incentives, and by encouraging a sense of loyalty to the organization and a devotion to duty. The problem, especially in industry and commerce where innovation is often essential, is to do this without developing an organization type to which all newcomers are expected to conform. Again it is a problem of balance, since there will always be a clash between the need for managers to be reliable and the dangers of over-conformity. Top management should assess whether it has the balance right between the advantages of reliability and the limitations of conformity. In weighing the scales it should allow for the fact that judgement is likely to be weighted against the individualist.

The conclusions we may draw from our discussion of bureaucracy are that it is bound to develop in an established and continuing organization that seeks to be efficient. Some degree of bureaucracy is essential for efficient management. The problem is how much? As organizations grow, they need to become more bureaucratic to ensure order in what is done, but the inherent dangers of bureaucracy need to be guarded against. A knowledge of what these are can help to prevent them. The amount of bureaucracy that is appropriate will vary with the particular circumstances of the organization. What these are, and how they do, and should, influence the organization and behaviour of management will be a

8. William H. Whyte's book, *The Organization Man*, was widely acclaimed in the mid-fifties for its vivid picture of the character and dangers of such conformity. Published by Simon and Schuster, New York, 1956, and Jonathan Cape, London, 1957.

recurring subject throughout this book. A general guide is that the greater the rate of change affecting the organization, the more adaptable it needs to be, and hence the less formal and bureaucratic.

SUMMARY

Bureaucracy provides a common setting – and one we often take for granted – for organizations with different purposes. (We used 'bureaucracy' with its sociological meaning of a particular form of organization, not in its pejorative sense.) The characteristics of a bureaucracy, which these organizations have in common, are, one, *specialization* of jobs, which become continuing posts for which suitably qualified individuals are recruited; two, an *hierarchy of authority* composed of clearly defined levels: three, a *system of rules*; and four, *impersonality*, which is seen both in the administration of the rules and in selection and promotion.

Bureaucracy has developed because it is more efficient than other forms of organization. It makes for rational and continuing administration. The increasing size and complexity of organizations encourages the growth of bureaucracy. So does the demand for equality of treatment. Bureaucracy also gains strength from the arguments of the advocates of scientific management, who urge the value of a carefully defined, orderly organization. Rapid change limits the growth of bureaucracy because a more flexible organization is needed to adapt to it.

For managers there are advantages and disadvantages in working in a bureaucracy. It suits some temperaments better than others. On the one hand, managers are freed from much former arbitrariness. They will be appointed for their experience and qualifications and, as far as possible, promoted on merit. They will have an established status with appropriate salary and privileges. They can look forward to a known pattern of career expectations. Their loyalty should be to the organization rather than to individuals. On the other hand, managers lose some of their freedom of action. They will be the occupant of a continuing position with prescribed duties and limitations within which they must work. If they are good, their speed of advancement may be less than in a more free-wheeling society.

The problems of bureaucracy are the problems of balance: how to have rules that are impersonal but not inhuman, that are fair yet take the individual into account; how to have a structure that is not too rigid to adjust to change; how to have loyal managers who further the organization's objectives without developing into organization men and women. These problems are inescapable, but they can be ameliorated.

6

What Kind of Structure?

Any manager needs to understand the main problems to be tackled in designing the formal structure of an organization. Few will have to plan a new organization but many will have some opportunities to make choices in how work is to be organized. They will benefit from knowing the pros and cons of different choices. So will managers who are having to cope with a reorganization, which is a common experience for most managers in large organizations. Understanding what is happening can help to reduce the stress. Being able to predict the likely consequences of an organizational change helps in managing it.

There are three aspects to an organization. There is the formal structure, which can be shown on an organization chart; there are the policies and procedures; and, more important than these two, there is people's behaviour within the organization. 'More important' because what people do will determine how well the organization works in practice. Yet the formal structure and the policies and procedures do matter, because they help to determine the kinds of jobs that people have, how they feel about their work, how easy it is to coordinate people's activities, and whether cooperation or conflict are encouraged.

This chapter is limited to the formal structure of the organization. It aims to:

1. Describe the main problems of organization and the kinds of decisions that have to be made in planning the structure.
2. Discuss what has been learnt from the study of structures in organizations and what relevance this has for the manager.[1]

We saw in the last chapter that the characteristics of a bureaucracy exist today, to a greater or lesser extent, in all large organizations and in most medium-sized ones, too. Yet they only provide the setting within which the organization will be designed. A hierarchy of authority and specialization of jobs are but the beginning. They do not provide the answer to two of the main problems of organization: how the work is to be divided – both between posts at the same levels and between different levels – and how it is to be coordinated. Once work is divided, there has to be coordination.

In any kind of organization, be it a company, a government department, a public enterprise, a hospital or a school, decisions have to be made about what work is to be done and how it is to be divided between jobs, and how jobs are to be grouped into sections, departments and even larger groupings. What kind of jobs to establish is so important a decision that it is discussed in a separate chapter in *The Reality of Organizations*. Here we shall look at the broader questions of the main types of work to be done and of how these are to be grouped together.

Division of Work

The first decision in a new organization is what are the main functions to be performed. In any company there are some obvious divisions. In a manufacturing company these will be production, marketing and sales, finance and personnel. Other functions are essential in some industries but not in others. A research department, for example, is vital to a company in a new, expanding and highly technical industry,

1. This can only be an introduction, concentrating on the classic studies. Readers wanting more information are referred to the author's companion volume, *The Reality of Organizations*, Macmillan and Pan.

such as electronics. New functions get added as organizations change or as new technology provides new ways of dealing with existing tasks. Computers and office technology are an example of how new technology can affect the division of work in many departments and in most organizations. There are more specialized examples, such as intensive care wards in hospitals.

The work of a company after being divided into the main functions, such as production and sales, is further subdivided into what are usually called line or operational and staff or specialist jobs. Line functions are those with direct responsibility for achieving the objectives of the organization. Staff activities are those that primarily exist to provide advice and service. Whether a function is line or staff should depend on the company's objectives. Research, for instance, is sometimes line when new products and processes are vital for the success of the company, or staff when its role is less important. As the company grows larger, and management finds it must hive off some of its activities, then more and more staff jobs are likely to be created: for example, market research, personnel and materials handling. Each of these may in turn grow by dividing into different specialities.

How to establish satisfactory relations between operational managers and staff personnel is a difficult problem of organization. It is difficult because of the possibilities of frustration and conflict that are always present in the relation. Managers may feel that their customary and well-tried ways of doing things are being threatened by new specialists, whose advice they may yet be afraid to ignore. They may become so unsure of their authority that they go to the specialist on even the smallest matter for a statement of 'Company Policy'. Alternatively, managers may pay no attention to the specialists, who may then feel frustrated by their lack of responsibility and frequent inability to get their ideas put into effect. The relation is often made more difficult by the specialist's jargon. There are usually fewer misunderstandings when the staff people report direct to an operational manager, but for some specialities this will be too expensive. Individual managers do not need their own lawyers, though a factory manager may well need a personnel officer.

Satisfactory relations between managers and specialists can only be achieved with time, which allows for the growth of mutual confidence. Hence, when management is planning a new organization, it cannot provide an answer to the problems of the relations between the two. It can, however, minimize the likelihood of trouble. The specialists should be located as near as possible to the manager whom they will be serving, so that mutual confidence can have the best chance of developing. Physical proximity is desirable, but where that is not convenient, good communications are essential.

One of the choices in the division of work is what is to be done within the organization by its regular employees, and what is to be done outside by using other firms and individual consultants. In many organizations this choice is greater than in the past because of the opportunities that information technology provides for linking those who are working from home. It makes easier the revival of cottage industry in its modern electronic form. Heavy industries like petrochemicals and oil refining have much less flexibility in what work they can put out than organizations whose main resource is people. Software firms, for example, can run on a small number of full-time staff and a variety of part-timers and those used for particular projects. Market research, public relations, catering and computing are examples of services required in many organizations that may be bought from outside.

Grouping of Work

In a simple organization it may be easy to decide what jobs should be grouped together, as the division of work between the major activities is clear. Production, sales and accounts will be needed in a simple manufacturing company. It is only as organizations get larger that choices have to be made. In sales, for example, a common choice is between organizing by product, so that salesmen are responsible for particular products, or by area, when the sales force is organized geographically. Organization by area is a common basis in government departments dealing directly with the public. The type of customer or client is another common basis for dividing up work. In companies there may be separate sales staff for important customers. In hospitals patients may be grouped together by sex, age, type of illness or the amount of care required.

How Many Tiers?

The number of tiers in the management hierarchy vary in practice from two in a small company to more than ten in some large companies. Size obviously makes a difference, but management still has considerable choice as to how many levels to establish. It may opt for as few tiers as possible, on the grounds that this makes for better communication and more responsible and interesting jobs. This would require either a wide span of control or a group type of organization that is divided into a number of smaller, semi-autonomous units. (The span of control is the number of people directly reporting to a manager.) It may prefer a larger number of tiers, arguing that the business does not lend itself to the creating of subsidiary companies, that a narrow span of control makes for better supervision, and that more tiers in the management hierarchy increase promotion opportunities.

Posts will have to be assigned to the different levels. In planning a new company this may be done by deciding what functions are sufficiently important to report to the managing director, what activities should report to the senior managers, and so on. In an established company there can be difficulties. If the place of individual managers in the hierarchy has always been hazy, an attempt to state it clearly may upset many people who believed their position to be higher. This problem most often arises when an organization chart is published. It is one reason why some top managers are opposed to organization charts, although they may have a hand-made copy locked in their desk, as a guide to how they would like the organization to be.

Organization Charts

Management should next decide whether it wants an organization chart and, if so, what kind. It might consider some of the attempts that have been made to draw charts that are more informative than the traditional ones. If its planning has been as methodical as our description, it will probably have roughed out a chart as it went along. The chart helps to show what has been decided. It will also be useful for showing to newly appointed managers and inquiring visitors. But organization charts have their dangers. Their usefulness is often exaggerated and they can rapidly get out of date. All too few organization charts have explanatory notes; without them readers may make different assumptions about their meaning. They may also be in danger of thinking the reality is as tidy as the chart (in the next chapter we shall see how far the two may be divorced). Unless charts are frequently revised, they may soon give a false picture of even the formal organization. In sum, an organization chart can be a useful tool, and an aid to explanation about the organization, but it is often misused. Its apparent clarity can be misleading.

At this stage in planning an organization the framework is complete, but the task is not finished. If, for instance, top management interviews a potential sales manager and shows the chart, the question that might and should be asked is 'How much responsibility shall I have?' This question would show up two areas that have yet to be tackled. One, what type of decisions should be taken at each level of management – that is, how much decentralization should there be? Two, what should be the responsibilities of each job?

Decentralization

One of the most difficult decisions to be made in planning or changing an organization is how much decentralization there should be. No business of any size is completely centralized, for if it is to work at all, some decisions must be taken on the spot rather than at the centre. The choice is not between centralization and decentralization but of how much decentralization there should be and what decisions should be made at different levels. The answer is likely to vary from one company to another, according to what decisions top management consider of vital importance to the business. In one company, for example, all proposed price changes have to be referred to top management. In another, pricing decisions will be made lower down.

What is the best balance between centralization and decentralization may well vary at different periods in a firm's history. In a new company, or in an amalgamation of two or more companies, greater centralization will be necessary in the early stages so as to establish common policies, where these are desired. A well-established management tradition will make greater decentralization easier, because managers will tend to think and act in the same way. The calibre of junior and middle management will also affect the amount of decentralization that is practicable. This is often one of the constraints on decentralization in developing countries. The structure of the company will help to encourage or discourage decentralization. A flat organization will encourage it because responsibility will be divided between fewer levels and because managers with many subordinates will have to leave more decisions to them.

Job Descriptions

A subject on which top management in one company may differ vigorously from that in another is the extent to which it is desirable to define the responsibilities of a job ('job description') and to specify the qualifications necessary to fill the particular job ('job specification'). At one extreme, top management might appoint a general sales manager and just leave it to him to sell the products. At the opposite extreme, before looking for a general sales manager, management draws up a careful job description and from that prepares a specification of the kind of person needed to fill it.

The illustrative job description given by Brech, an ardent advocate of the value of these descriptions, for such a post lists forty-nine responsibilities, which include, for instance:

25 Taking up with the Managing Director, and/or the General Production Manager, any matters which prevent the smooth coordination of Manufacturing and Sales;

41   Providing general supervision of the work of the Export Department to ensure conformity with policy and programme, the maintenance of the Company's standards and reputation, and keeping expenditure within budgeted limits;

48   Encouraging Sales Supervisors, Engineers and Agents to offer constructive suggestions in regard to improvements of the Company's products.[2]

One argument used in favour of the first approach, that is, leaving the scope of the job up to the individual, is that if you appoint people with initiative, they will be able to make their own jobs and should not be limited in doing so by being given precise terms of reference. Another is that in most companies conditions are always changing; therefore, any attempt to define precisely the responsibilities attached to jobs is bound to become rapidly out-dated. Those who support the second approach argue that definition of responsibilities is essential if top management is to make certain that no aspect of the work is overlooked because nobody is clearly responsible for doing it. It is also suggested that much personal friction can be avoided if people know exactly what they are responsible for and to whom.

The difference in these two approaches reflects a difference in management philosophy. Detailed job descriptions will be supported by those who believe in the virtues of order and of control. The other approach will be favoured by those who emphasize initiative and flexibility. The relative importance of these priorities will vary with the purposes and current position of the organization. Some do require more flexibility than others. Even so, top management will tend to favour one approach or the other.

Reorganization

So far we have discussed the organizational decisions that must be made when planning a new company. It is easier to describe the kind of decisions that have to be made then. Yet

2. Brech, E. F. L., *Organization: The Framework of Management*, 2nd edition, pp. 222–3, Longman, London, 1965.

the establishment of a new company that is large enough to
have a formal management structure is a comparatively rare
event. The reorganization of existing companies is much more
common, and many of the same considerations will apply.
All of them will have to be examined if a really thorough
reorganization is being planned. Companies change: the conditions in which they operate may alter, they may expand,
change their products, gradually acquire a different type of
management, and so on. Any or all of these may be reasons
why the existing organization no longer seems satisfactory.
Many companies have grown piecemeal, often, at least to
some extent, around personalities. The posts that were developed by the abilities and weaknesses of particular people
may continue after they have left. At times in a company's
development, management will feel a need to re-examine the
organization. Then, as in the company that is being planned
before it is established, management may ask the question:
'What principles, or at least guidelines, are there in planning
an efficient organization?' and perhaps, even more specific-
ally, 'Is there a best way of organizing?'

It is not only companies that have periodic reorganizations.
Growth or decline can necessitate a reorganization in other
bodies. Many public organizations are changed because their
new political masters have different views about what they
should be doing. In any type of organization top management or a committee of enquiry may decide that a change
must surely be an improvement on the all too visible problems of the present organization.

One Best Way to Organize?

Managers today get very different advice from writers on
management from that given by many writers in the first half
of the century and even into the fifties. Then management
pundits like Urwick[3] looked for and described universal
principles that could be applied in designing any organization. Urwick, whose work was respected on both sides of the

3. Urwick, L., Notes on the Theory of Organization, American Management Association, New York, 1952.

Atlantic, listed ten principles of good organization.[4] Now organization textbooks do not offer universal principles, though some suggest guidelines. This change originated in the studies by social scientists of how organizations work in practice, which showed that universal principles are not valid.

The idea of span of control is a good example of the move from a principle to a guideline. This was Urwick's eighth principle of organizing: 'No person should supervise more than five, or at the most, six direct subordinates whose work interlocks.'

The argument used to support it was that no individual could understand the relations between more than five or six people if their work was related. However, studies showed that in practice there is a wide range in the number of subordinates reporting to a manager. An American study examined the span of control of the chief executives of 620 manufacturing companies in Ohio with 100 or more employees. (Chief executives also included managers of branch plants.) These companies covered a very wide range of industries. This study showed that the average span of control of the chief executive increased as the number of employees went up. In the firms studied that had 1,400 to 3,000 employees the most frequent span was eight subordinates; in firms with over 3,000 employees it was nine. In these larger firms 62.7 per cent of all the main–plant executives had a span of seven or more subordinates. In the plants with less than 1,500 employees the most common spans were four, five or six subordinates. The span of control was also found to vary according to the type of industry. Higher spans were more common in the main plants of paper and allied products, of petroleum and coal; in branch plants they were more common for stone, clay and glass products, electrical machinery equipment and supplies, and miscellaneous manufacturing.[5]

Another American study, this time of the number of

4. ibid.
5. Healey, James H., *Executive Coordination and Control*, Ohio Bureau of Business Research, College of Commerce and Administration, The Ohio State University, 1956.

executives reporting to the chief executive in 100 companies employing over 5,000 people, yielded similar results. All the firms included in this study were described by the American Management Association as having good management practices. The median number of subordinates was between eight and nine and the range from one to twenty-four. The chief executives of twenty-four firms had thirteen or more subordinates reporting directly to them.[6]

These studies all looked at the average span of control. Once the wide variations that existed in practice had been discovered, there was a need for research that would help to explain the reasons for these differences. Joan Woodward found that the span of the chief executives in the 100 manufacturing companies that she studied varied directly with the sophistication of the technology employed. It was four in unit production firms, seven in mass production companies and ten in process production. Companies with below average success rates had spans of control that were significantly above or below the median. She also found wide variations in the span of the first line supervisor: an average of twenty-three in unit production firms, forty-nine in large batch and mass production and thirteen in process industries.[7]

Another study, of the span of control of the head of marketing and sales in sixty-seven manufacturing companies in the US, examined what factors were associated with high or low spans of control. It found that a relatively large span of control was found where the functions supervised were similar, subordinates were in different locations (explained by the similarity of their jobs), personal assistants were used, and the subordinates had considerable experience in the job.[8]

A comparative study of a number of industrial organizations in different European countries suggested further factors that may affect the span of control in practice and make a

6. Dale, Ernest, 'Planning and Developing the Company Organization Structure, *Research Report No. 20*, pp. 56–8, American Management Association, New York, 1952.

7. Woodward, Joan, *Industrial Organization: Theory and Practice*, Oxford University Press, London, 1965.

8. Udell, John G., 'An Empirical Test of Hypotheses Relating to Span of Control', *Administrative Science Quarterly*, December 1967.

comparison of the average span of control rather unrealistic.[9] One is the use of staff assistants to relieve the line manager and thus make possible a wider span of control. In practice they may function as an intervening level of management, although this is rarely shown on organization charts. Another factor is the extent and quality of lateral communications; where these are well developed, much of the coordination may be done by the subordinates themselves without reference to their manager. This will lighten his load and make possible a wider span of control. The research also showed that the actual span of control is sometimes different from that shown on the organization chart, as managers may encourage people other than their immediate subordinates to discuss problems with them. They may take a particular interest in one function, such as training, although the training officer is shown on the chart several levels below.

A distinction should, therefore, be made between the number of people who are supervised, that is, who report directly to the superior, and the number who have access to the manager. In particular, access to the chief executive, which can be an important factor in morale, will take up the superior's time and may, therefore, make a small span of direct control 'reasonable'.

These different studies show that the principle of a specific span of control is unrealistic. In practice the formal span of control varies considerably. As a guideline it is still worth considering whether the span of control is too wide, but finding the answer is not simple. Those who supervise people whose work is not interconnected, like retail chain store managers or post office managers, can have more subordinates than those who have to worry about the interrelations of their work and personality.

The burden imposed on managers by a particular number of subordinates depends on a great variety of factors, including temperamental characteristics, such as the extent to which they can be frequently interrupted without becoming

9. European Productivity Agency, 'A Study of Post-War Growth in Management Organizations: Comparison of Chemical and Engineering Firms in Eight Western European Countries', *Project No. 347*, pp. 11–14.

upset; questions of ability both of the superior and of the subordinates; the physical location and the nature of the work, including the type and frequency of the decisions that have to be made; and the strength of informal organization. The latter can reduce the pressure on the manager, as subordinates may coordinate much of the work themselves.

The phrase 'span of control' is itself questionable, as it suggests the need for much more direct supervision than may be necessary. Subordinates may be experienced, well-motivated and capable of coordinating much of their own work. Their boss may need to spend very little time with them and then mainly for the exchange of information. The role that the boss needs to play in relation to subordinates is one of the factors that is relevant to deciding how many direct subordinates would be too many.

What Social Scientists have Contributed

The approach of social scientists to the study of organizations is almost bewilderingly varied. As Mason Haire pointed out, a parallel would be the fable of the blind men decribing an elephant.

> There is little doubt here that it is a single elephant being discussed, but, by and large, each of the observers begins the description from a different point, and often with a special end in view. Each of the authors is dealing with organizations and how they work; but, to some extent, they start from different bases and have different things in mind which need explaining.[10]

The contribution of social scientists can be illustrated by a few of the studies that are recognized as classic ones. An example of a study that is of direct help in planning the organization of a particular function is that by Professor Herbert Simon and three colleagues, which sought to expand our knowledge about human behaviour in organizations, and to do this in a way that would cast light on the specific

10. Haire, Mason (ed.), *Modern Organization Theory: A Symposium of the Foundation for Research on Human Behaviour*, p. 2, John Wiley, New York, 1959, and Chapman and Hall, London, 1959.

problems of organizing effectively the controller's department in large companies.[11] ('Controller' is the American term
for the head of the accounting department.) They defined
an effective accounting department as one that provided
information of high quality, did so at a minimum cost, and
facilitated the long-range development of competent accounting executives. The research workers studied seven large
companies that were geographically dispersed. These were in
a variety of industries and differed in the extent to which
they centralized or decentralized their accounting departments. The research was carried out by interviews, by
studying accounting reports and, to a limited extent, by
observation.

The research workers found that in each of the companies
accounting information was used at various levels to answer
three different kinds of question: one, score-card, 'how am I
doing?'; two, attention-directing, 'what problems shall I look
into?'; and three, problem-solving, 'which course of action is
better?' The type of information needed varied at different
levels of the organization. The extent to which the information was used depended mainly on how close was the relation
between the accountants as sources of information and the
managers as consumers. To achieve this close relation, different pattens of organization were needed for the different
types of information.

The research showed that there is no such general thing as
accounting information. Therefore, in designing the organization of an accounting department one must think of a
number of types of data that need different channels of communication if they are to be most useful. The research team
concluded that there are three major divisions in the accounting function, each of which can be separated from the others.
These are record-keeping, current analysis, and special studies
for problem-solving purposes. The research workers said
that:

---

11. Simon, Herbert A., Guetzhow, H., Kozmetsky, G., Tyndall, G.,
Centralization v. Decentralization in Organizing the Controller's Department,
Controllership Foundation Inc., New York, 1954. Reissued 1978, Scholars
Book, Houston, Texas, Accounting Classic Series.

Combining the functions leads to a potential conflict between the accountant's function of providing service to operating departments, and his function of analysing operations to provide valid and objective data for higher levels of management. Separating the record–keeping functions from analytical work is also an important supplement to an effective internal audit in reducing the dangers of collusion. It may also give the analytical personnel greater freedom to develop close working relationships with operating executives without a feeling of conflicting responsibilities.

Another reason for separating the functions is to allow greater flexibility for organizing each of them in the most economical and effective manner . . . Each can be centralized or decentralized to the extent that appears desirable, independently of the others.[12]

The above is an example of a study with immediate practical application. It shows how the organization should be designed to meet the needs of those concerned.

The most important contributions of social scientists to our understanding of organizations is showing that different types of business need different forms of organization and that the appropriate kind of organization can change with the company's situation. Two studies in the UK in the 1950s helped to shatter the idea that there are universal principles of organizing.

Joan Woodward studied 100 manufacturing firms in SE Essex and found a great variety of types of organization.[13] She concluded that the variation could be explained by the type of production. The three main methods – unique and small batch, mass, and process – all needed their own distinctive forms of organization. Peter Drucker pointed out some of the organizational implications of the differences in types of production:

Under unique-product production, management can be centralized at the top. Coordination between the various functions is

12. ibid., p. 5.
13. Woodward, Joan, 'Management and Technology', *Problems of Progress in Industry*, No. 3, p. 37. Department of Scientific and Industrial Research, HMSO, London, 1958.

needed primarily at the top. Selling, design, engineering, and production, can all be distinct and need only come together where company policy is being determined. It is this pattern of unique product production that is still largely assumed in our organization theory – even though unique product production may well be the exception rather than the rule in the majority of American industries today.

Mass production 'old style' can still maintain this pattern, though with considerable difficulty and at a high price in efficiency. It does better with a pattern that establishes centres of decision and integration much further down. For it requires close coordination between the engineers who design the product, the production people who make it, the sales people who market it, and so forth.

In both mass production 'new style' and process production, functional centralization is impossible. They require the closest cooperation from people from all functions at every stage . . . And decisions affecting the business as a whole have to be taken at a decentralized level – sometimes at a level not even considered 'management' today.[14]

By mass production 'old style' Drucker means the manufacture of uniform products in large quantity. By mass production 'new style' he means the manufacture of uniform parts that are then mass-assembled into many different products.

The second major study which showed how different situations require different forms of organization was that by Burns and Stalker. They compared companies in the electronics industry that were going through a rapid change with a firm producing rayon filament yarn, which had become a routine production. This comparison suggested that the amount of change affecting the organization influenced the extent of its flexibility. The research workers distinguished two contrasting types of oranization: one they called 'mechanistic', which means suitable for stable conditions; the other 'organic', which means adapted to changing conditions. The

14. Drucker, Peter F., *The Practice of Management*, op. cit., pp. 90–1.

firm making rayon filament yarn was an example of a mechanistic organization, in it each person:

> . . . knew just what he could do in normal circumstances without consulting anyone else; just what point of deviation from the normal he should regard as the limit of his competence; and just what he should do when this limit was reached – i.e., report to his superior. The whole system was devised to preserve normality and stability. The downward flow of instructions and orders, and the upward flow of reports and requests for such instructions and orders, were precisely and clearly channelled; it had the characteristics of a smoothly working automatic machine. Since everyone knew both his job and its limits, there was little consultation; contacts ran up and down, from subordinate to superior and vice versa, and the great majority of those contacts resulted in the giving of definite orders. The outstanding characteristic of the structure was that it was mechanical and authoritarian. And it worked very well.[15]

In stable conditions, such as those operating in this company, the organization can be treated as a mechanical structure. In it each job has precisely defined rights and duties and technical requirements. The knowledge of the firm's needs and situation is concentrated at the top, thus making possible a hierarchic, authoritarian form of management structure. When a company is operating in conditions of rapid change, it must be much more flexible and have what Burns and Stalker called an organic system: that is, one in which the boundaries of jobs are fluid and there is more consultation and exchange of information than commands. Interaction between people also takes place laterally as much as vertically. Each of these types of organization suit their different conditions.

Later research by Lawrence and Lorsch made a further contribution to what is now called 'contingency theory', that is, the theory that the nature of the organization is contingent

15. Croome, Honor, 'Human Problems of Innovation, based on a study by Burns, Tom and Stalker, G. M., *Problems of Progress in Industry*, No. 5, p. 12, Department of Scientific and Industrial Research, HMSO, London, 1960.

upon its situation.[16] They examined the effect of different
environments, in particular the amount of instability and
variety, upon the structure and working of organizations.
They showed that the nature of the environment affected two
oranizational tasks, that of *differentiation* between tasks and
that of the *integration* of the separate tasks or functions. They
found that in complex and dynamic environments there was
a greater need for differentiation than in simpler, more stable
ones, and the greater the differentiation, the more complex
had to become the methods of integration. Greater differentiation of functions led to differences in the attitudes and
behaviour of managers in each function. They had different
objectives, different time orientations and generally dealt
with their colleagues in different ways. Lawrence and
Lorsch's study is an illustration of the way in which the
structure of the organization affects the behaviour of individuals, a subject that we shall examine in the next chapter.

What these, and other, research reports indicate is that
there is no one ideal form of organization; hence no universally applicable set of principles, except of the most general
kind. The organization will vary according to the needs of
the company, which will depend upon its situation. Management, therefore, needs to examine the company's objectives,
and its current situation, before designing or changing the
pattern of organization. This is true for management in any
kind of organization.

SUMMARY

In this chapter we examined the problems that face managers
in designing a new organization or modifying an old one; and
considered the help they might get from writers on organization. We outlined the different decisions that have to be made
in planning an organization. First is the division of work,
which depends upon the objectives of the organization. Second
is the further subdivision into line or operational and staff or

16. Lawrence, Paul R. and Lorsch, Jay W., *Organization and Environment, Managing Differentiation and Integration*, Harvard University, Division
of Research, Graduate School of Business Administration, Boston, 1967.

specialist jobs: the former have direct responsibility for results, the latter exist primarily to provide service and advice. The relation between the two is a perennial problem of organization. It must be based on mutual confidence, but organizational arrangements can help to promote it. The third is the question of how many levels of authority there should be. Management has to decide whether it wants to limit these to the smallest number possible. For the fourth we looked at the usefulness of organization charts and decided that they could be a useful tool, but one that is often abused. The limitations of such charts were stressed. The fifth is one of the most difficult decisions in planning an organization: how much decentralization there should be. This varies at different periods in the company's history, depending in part on the extent to which common policies exist or are desired. The calibre of junior and middle management and the type of decisions to be made were among the other factors that affect how much decentralization there should be. In the sixth we examined the arguments for and against job descriptions. Their use depends both upon management philosophy and upon the rapidity of change.

Social scientists since the 1950s have studied how organizations work in practice. They have found a great variety of types of organization and have sought to explain these differences. Some of their findings are of direct relevance for managers. One of the most important is that there is no one ideal form of organization, hence no universally applicable set of principles for its design. Instead the organization must be designed in accordance with its needs as these are determined by the situation.

When management is planning an organization, whether of a company as a whole or of an individual department, it needs to analyse both the objectives of the company and the demands of the situation. It should also check at intervals whether the organization is meeting changing needs.

7

People and Organization

So far we have discussed the organization without the people who will bring it to life, make it work, and give it its distinctive character. Now we need to look at how people may influence the formal structure, as well as how the latter may affect people's behaviour by the demands it makes on them and the strains it imposes. First, let us look at an organization as seen through the eyes of a newly recruited manager and then more broadly at the social relations within an organization.

Learning the Ropes

Managers joining a new company would soon make a gaffe if they relied upon the formal organization as their only guide to how the organization worked. The organization chart may embody management's intentions, but this planned structure is run by people and they will have an effect on how it works in practice. The formal organization does not, and cannot, show all the relationships that grow up between people; though in static conditions it will be more likely to do so than in periods of rapid change. An understanding of how the organization actually works is more necessary for the managers than a knowledge of the formal structure. Hence managers who move from one firm to another and, to a lesser extent, even from one department to another, will need time to learn how people work together. Only then will they know the best way to achieve what they want. They must find out, if they are to work effectively and to get on, how the status order differs from that shown on the chart; who takes the lead, and in what circumstances, and who follows. They must also be sensitive to the power politics, to whether management is divided into cliques and, if so, how the cliques are made up and what their relation is to each other. Then they will need to know whom they must get on their side if they wish to sell an idea. In one company it will usually be sufficient to get the support of the managing director. In another, subordinates as well as colleagues may need to be in agreement.

There may be one or two influential people, not necessarily the most senior, whose opinion can sway the others. The ways of finding out what is happening in a company will also vary. In some there may be committees and informal meetings for the exchange of information; in others the managers' dining-room may be the best source of news. In most companies there will be one or more people who are particularly well-informed about what is happening – 'Ask old Bill, he will know.' On the shop floor the best place for information may be the lavatory – a useful source for the social research worker but of no use to the manager, who will usually be closeted in a separate place. Women managers can be at a disadvantage. In many firms one finds attractive new washrooms to provide for the advent of women in previously all-male managements. The women gain in privacy but lose in the opportunities for informal talk.

New managers have to learn the dos and don'ts, the unwritten rules, which may well be different from those in their previous organization. They must learn when they can write or ring and when they must go and see the person if they want information. In some companies, acceptance by colleagues may partly depend on conversation in the managers' dining-room, and they should know what topics are taboo. Dress may still be subject to some important don'ts – recently in one company when a man asked why he did not get an annual salary increase, he was told that it was because he had worn a sweater instead of a jacket, which 'showed that he was obviously not taking his management position seriously'. The ambitious manager will want to know what are the standards of 'taking one's job seriously'. In this example dress was important; elsewhere it may be getting to one's desk early or staying late. But in a few – all too few – companies habitual overtime may be judged a sign of inefficiency. All these informal customs and procedures will help to give an organization its character, will make it different from another company that has the same formal structure. These the new managers must learn before they can become effective members of the management team. They will benefit from a general understanding of how people work together in an organization, but they will also need the detailed knowledge of how their particular organization works, because as Pettigrew says: 'Those who accurately understand how a structure operates are in a much better position to make it work to their advantage than others.'[1]

How People Work Together

When people work together, they establish social relationships and customary ways of doing things. This can be called the informal organization, that is, the patterns of behaviour that get established. It is not the behaviour that is described in any organization manual or suggested by any organization chart. How people work together in practice cannot be laid down in even the most comprehensive job descriptions, as it will depend, at least in part, upon the relations that develop between people – hence, on the kind of people they are, their particular strengths and weaknesses and how they react to each other. Therefore, an organization is not just a collection of isolated individuals performing the specific functions of their allotted jobs. It is also a set of social relations made up of how A reacts to B and both of them to C, of social groups that influence the attitudes and actions of their members and, sometimes, also of a number of cliques or factions – groups

1. Pettigrew, Andrew M., *The Politics of Organizational Decision-Making*, op. cit., p. 274.

that are organized against others. Two things tend to happen when people work together: they may form social groups and they may develop informal methods of getting their work done, that is, informal organization. Both of these can have important effects on efficiency.

When several people work in close contact with each other for any length of time, they are likely to become a social group. They are then more than a collection of individuals who happen to be working together, and acquire a sense of identity as a group in which some people are inside and others outside. There may be several social groups within one large work group and some individuals who do not belong to a group. The social group will have a sense of like-mindedness among its members and will agree on many subjects of immediate importance to them. What they agree on will depend upon the purposes the group serves.

The cohesiveness that members of a social group develop can have great strengths. The social support that comes from a close-knit group can be exciting and encourage what would otherwise seem a superhuman effort. It brings dangers too: 'we belong, others are outsiders'. This can be the basis for fruitful competition, fruitful in that all try harder to do well and to win, but it can also lead to antagonism and to lack of cooperation. Hence managers need to be aware of the power and the dangers of social groups. Good managers provide the climate in which groups want to pursue aims that match their own. Good managers, too, organize work so that those who need to cooperate with each other have opportunities to become friendly rather than to see each other as the enemy.

This tendency for people who work together to develop social groups has important implications for management, as it can materially assist or considerably handicap management objectives. A number of studies have shown that enthusiasm for work is much greater where group affiliations have been built up, provided the aims of the group do not run counter to those of management. People enjoy their work more, and are less likely to be absent from work, because they have become part of a social group in which they are important as a person.

Informal groups within the formal organization can also work against management aims. Numerous research projects have shown that, even with an incentive scheme, workers will not necessarily aim at the highest output they can achieve. Instead a group of workers may establish their own output norm, which may well be considerably less than that which could be maintained by the fastest worker, and even less than that of an average worker. The group may establish quite elaborate procedures for ensuring that this norm is obtained but not exceeded, including various forms of pressure to ensure that no individual exceeds the norm.

The informal group will have its own aims, which may support or oppose management aims. It will also have its own sanctions, which will differ from those in the formal organization: these will consist of the withdrawal of acceptance and help by the group. The degree to which this is done will depend upon the heinousness of the infringement of the group's aims. In extreme cases the individual may be ostracized. When the informal group is strong, its sanctions are likely to be more compelling on a group member than those of management, since they are more certain to be applied. Management may not catch a culprit who is violating one of the official rules, but the informal group is much more likely to know if one of its members breaks its social code.

One of the greatest advantages of a group is to facilitate coordination. Its self-disciplining and self-checking means that far less management time and effort are necessary to ensure that work is being carried out satisfactorily. But this is only valuable where the group is working to further management aims. Whether the informal group will work with or against management aims will depend upon whether or not management has gained the staff's commitment. This is such an important subject for any manager that it was discussed in Chapter 3, 'Getting the Job Done'.

All organizations develop informal methods for getting work done, and these may facilitate or oppose management aims. The importance of informal organization has long been recognized. Chester Barnard, an American executive writing in the 1930s, said that its functions at the management level are:

The communication of intangible facts, opinions, suggestions, suspicions, that cannot pass through formal channels without raising issues calling for decisions, without dissipating dignity and objective authority, and without overloading executive positions; also to minimize excessive cliques of political types arising from too great divergence of interest and views; to promote self-discipline of the group; and to make possible the development of important personal influences in the organization.[2]

Hence informal organization can serve to sift information and ideas before they go to formal authority. Many things, too, can be done informally, often with the knowledge and agreement of senior management, which it would be embarrassing to acknowledge as official policy. As Perrin Stryker put it:

> The informal organization that pervades every company is so complex that it probably could never be completely charted. But it is this hidden operating structure that gets the work done. Indeed, it is the biggest intangible asset – and usually the touchiest open secret of any management.[3]

We so often take informal organization for granted that we tend to talk as if it did not exist. Many top managers when asked about the organization of their company would describe the formal organization without adding any reservations about the way it operates in practice. A description of how top management worked in a medium-sized company will illustrate some of the differences between the formal and informal organization. The organization chart puts all the senior managers who reported to the managing director on the same level.

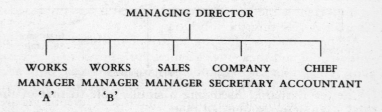

2. Barnard, Chester, *The Functions of the Executive*, op. cit., p. 225.
3. Stryker, Perrin and editors of *Fortune*, *A Guide to Modern Management Methods*, p. 108, McGraw-Hill, New York, 1954.

Preliminary inquiries soon showed that the managing director's subordinates were not all departmental heads of equal importance. The sales manager was really only a clerk, since the managing director took a strong personal interest in sales and in effect acted as the sales manager, playing an active part in the day-to-day running of the department. It would not take much time to discover the actual status and responsibility of the sales manager, but it would probably need some experience of how this top management worked in practice to find out that one of these senior managers, the chief accountant, was the most important. He was frequently consulted by the managing director on many aspects of the business and was also used by his colleagues, because his advice carried weight with the managing director, to interpret their grievances or ideas to him. The actual role of the chief accountant could not have been guessed at by looking at the organization chart. A more realistic picture of status and communication in this company is shown in the chart below. The dotted lines show the second channel for communication. The chief accountant is not put in a direct line between the managing director and the other top managers, as he does not function, either officially or unofficially, as the assistant managing director but merely as adviser and interpreter.

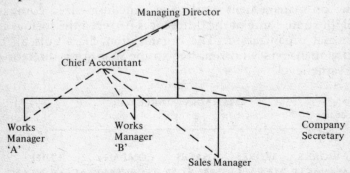

Chester Barnard, discussing a similar role to that of the chief accountant, suggested that:

> . . . many men not only exercise beneficent influence far beyond that implied by their formal status, but most of them, at the

time, would lose their influence if they had corresponding formal status. The reason may be that men may have personal qualifications of high order that will not operate under the stress of commensurate official responsibility.[4]

Such a manager can help to reduce the isolation of the chief executive, by acting as a trusted go-between who carries messages to and from the heights. In the example given above, top management worked more efficiently because the role played by the chief accountant helped to offset the managing director's weaknesses in dealing with his subordinates. The success of the chief accountant's role was, however, based on trust; the other top managers found that it was easier to get the managing director to listen to what they wanted if they could persuade the chief accountant to sell their ideas or to explain their grievances for them, and they trusted him to put them forward in good faith. The managing director also trusted the advice of the chief accountant. Such a relation can only work harmoniously where there is an absence of personal animosity. (In our example this was helped by the futility of competition for the managing director's post. It was a family firm where the managing director would be succeeded by his son.) Where there are personality clashes, cliques may develop, which can be harmful to efficiency. If, for instance, the other managers had not trusted the chief accountant, they would have resented his close relations with the managing director and might have banded together and given him only the minimum cooperation.

Informal organization may also develop to by-pass or to protect an inefficient individual or group. In one company, for instance, as other departments found that the sales control department was inaccurate and behind in its work, they gradually took to doing the work themselves, but routing the final estimates through the sales department. Senior management was unaware of what was happening and nobody would tell them for fear of getting their colleagues in sales control into trouble. In this example good relations masked

4. op. cit., p. 226.

inefficiency. This may often happen when colleagues seek to cover up the slowness or inefficiency of one of their number. Such 'covering up' need not necessarily stem from antagonism to management. Sometimes, of course, it does, especially on the shop floor.

Informal organization may also grow up because rapid change makes the formal organization out-of-date. Initially, in changing conditions people will try to solve problems on an *ad hoc* basis as they arise but, sooner or later, if the formal organization is not adapted to meet the new situation, they will develop informal organization to cope. If, for instance, interdepartmental meetings are not set up to keep people in the picture, managers from different departments may make a habit of dropping in to a local pub once or twice a week to try, as one manager put it, 'to sort out the chaos'. The tendency of people to develop informal methods of coping with change has probably saved many companies that have failed to adapt their formal structure to radical changes in their environment.

How the Organization Affects People

People may modify the formal organization, but it is a reciprocal influence, for the organization also affects the behaviour of individuals and groups. It can impose pressures on people in particular jobs that may lead them to adopt informal means of trying to avoid, or lessen, the problems of their position. The influence of the organization on the behaviour of individuals is most clearly seen when people in the same jobs in different parts of the organization are found to react in similar ways. A study by Ralph H. Turner,[5] of the disbursement officer in the American Navy (supply officer), illustrates organizational pressures on particular jobs and how people may react to them. Similar examples can be found today in many other organizations. Turner found that the particular problems of the disbursement officer's job were, one, possible conflicts between regulations governing his

5. 'The Navy Disbursing Officer as a Bureaucrat', *American Sociological Review*, Vol. 12, pp. 342–8, June 1947.

function and orders from his superior, both of which were supposed to be obeyed; two, the fact that he held a lower rank than that of many of his clients; and three, pressure from people with whom he was in close contact and who wanted him to interpret the regulations in their favour. The last was made more difficult by a well-developed informal system for the exchange of favours, so that it was often hard for a man to get the services and equipment essential for his job, quite apart from personal goods, unless he could promise some return. If the disbursement officer stuck to the strictly formal procedure, he lost his potentially strong position in the system of mutual benefits. According to Ralph Turner:

> Two general tendencies emerge among disbursing officers as the consequences of orders conflicting with regulations and the pressures of rank and informal structure. One is differential treatment of clientele. Because of the time consumed in extra routine treatment of persons on the 'in', others get summary treatment. The second tendency is for loop-holes in regulations to become tools in the hand of the disbursing officer to elevate his own status. Thus he may become more concerned with his own bargaining power than with correct application of the rules.[6]

Another illustration of how people subject to the same organizational pressures may react in the same way comes from a study of the relations between production and inspection. This is a potentially difficult relation because of the criticism inherent in inspection. McKenzie and Pugh, who studied the relations between the two in a number of factories, found that where the two activities were organizationally separate, there tended to be a consistent pattern of comments at all levels in production. All would query the inspector's technical knowledge, complain that an important job was stopped, say that the criticized dimensions were irrelevant to the product's ultimate function and that, in general, the inspector did not understand production difficulties. The authors suggest that if 'the relation between inspection

6. ibid., pp. 347–8.

and production is organized in a given way, then certain pressures will occur and certain attitudes, comments and complaints will appear'.[7]

An example of one occupational group being viewed with suspicion by others is provided by a study of management accountants. In this study one manager said:

> The accounting system is geared to meet the needs of the board. It's a control instrument . . . my needs are different . . . I need the information for management . . . but it's too imperfect . . . but the board get it so we must be ready with answers to questions on variances.[8]

This manager illustrated the defensive reactions that accounting procedures can arouse. In one department studied the distrust of the accountants and their figures was so great that managers ran their own accounting system to provide information for decisions and to challenge the information provided by the accountants.

These, and other studies, show that many reactions that are put down to individual cussedness are due to pressures imposed by the situation in which the person has to work: pressures that are likely to produce a similar reaction in people of very different personalities. These are important findings, for they show that managers need to think more of the strains that may result from the form of organization. Problems are usually discussed in terms of personality, but the remedy may be to change the organization rather than the people. Several studies also show that the nature of the technological organization can have important effects on social relations in the working group. It can determine the amount and type of social contact that people can have with one another, hence the likelihood of social groups and satisfying relations developing.

The classic study by Walker and Guest of assembly line

7. McKenzie, R. M. and Pugh, D. S., 'Some Human Aspects of Inspection', *The Institution of Production Engineers Journal*, Vol. 36, No. 6, pp. 378–87, June 1957.

8. Hopper, T. M., 'Role Conflicts of Management Accountants and Their Position Within Organization Structures', *Accounting, Organizations and Society*, Vol. 5, No. 4, p. 408, 1980.

workers in a car factory showed that the technological layout and the high noise level imposed considerable restrictions on the amount of contact workers could have with one another. It also largely determined the amount and type of contact they had with supervision.[9] A study by the Tavistock Institute of Human Relations of different methods of coal-getting showed that a change in the method had radically altered the kind of social relations that had developed in association with the old method.[10] In another report by the Tavistock Institute of Human Relations on different methods of coal-getting[11] the research workers found striking differences between output, costs, and absenteeism for two methods of work organization. For instance, the absenteeism rate from all causes was 20 per cent of possible shifts under one method and 8.2 per cent under another. Both studies suggest that the method of work organization prevented the worker from establishing satisfactory social relations, which is likely to be bad for morale.

Professor Argyris, a well-known American writer on human relations, has attacked the traditional shop-floor organization for the demands it makes on the worker. He suggests that informal organization for restriction of output is a result of an inherent conflict between the demands of the formal organization and the needs of a psychologically healthy individual.[12] He argues that formal organization based on principles of task specialization, unity of direction, chain of command, and span of control, demands that the worker shall be dependent, subordinate and passive towards the leader. This will make psychologically healthy people – by that Argyris primarily means mature – feel failure,

9. Walker, Charles R. and Guest, Robert H., *The Foreman on the Assembly Line*, Harvard University Press, Cambridge, Mass, 1952.

10. Trist, E. L., and Bamforth, K. W., 'Some Social and Psychological Consequences of the Longwall Method of Coal-Getting', *Human Relations*, Vol. 4, No. 1, pp. 3–38, 1951.

11. Emery, F. E. and Trist, E. L., 'Socio-Technical Systems', *Management Sciences: Models and Techniques*, Vol. 11, p. 81, Pergamon Press, London, 1960.

12. Argyris, Chris, *Integrating the Individual and the Organization*, John Wiley, New York, 1964.

frustration and conflict. They will also develop a short-term view, whereas a mature person looks further ahead.

Workers may seek to adjust themselves to the conflict between their needs to be active, creative, and independent and the demands of the organization by leaving the company, by working hard to climb the ladder to a position where conditions are less frustrating, or for those for whom the first two options are too difficult or unappealing by becoming apathetic and aggressive. This will show itself in a loss of interest in work and in a desire to 'get even' with management. It may result in industrial disputes and restriction of output, slowing-down and goldbricking (secretly stockpiling finished work so that workers may have as much time as possible in which to do what they like). Informal work groups can sanction and perpetuate these methods of adaptation.

Restriction of output is widespread. It is important to try to understand the reasons. England, according to J. A. C. Brown, could increase her national income by one-half within five years if employee apathy was decreased.[13] He was writing in the early fifties, but the need to release the energy of individuals and of working groups remains as true today.[14] So important is it that the different approaches to doing so was the major subject of Chapter 3, 'Getting the Job Done'.

SUMMARY

The structure of an organization is modified by the people who work in it, so that even otherwise identical organizations will develop their own distinctive characters. People will develop their own ways of working together, which is called the 'informal organization'. This can be a great asset, as it can make allowances for personalities, adapt to change and

13. Brown, J. A. C., *The Social Psychology of Industry*, p. 87, Penguin Books, Harmondsworth, Middx, 1954.
14. Owen, Trevor, *Making Organizations Work*, Martinus Nijhoff, Leiden, 1978, writes perceptively about the need to release the sources of energy within the organization.

facilitate coordination. The social groups that tend to develop among those working closely together may be an important factor in promoting good morale, because people will then find their work more socially satisfying. Social groups may also work against management aims: for instance, when a group of workers develops its own informal organization to restrict output. Morale may be high, but because of the common cause of defeating management's objectives.

The relation between the formal organization and people is a reciprocal one. People modify the working of the formal organization, but their behaviour is also influenced by it. It may make demands on them which they find an undue strain, so that they seek ways of modifying these pressures. The method of work organization can determine how people relate to one another, which may affect both their productivity and their morale. Managers, therefore, need to be conscious of the ways in which methods of work organization may influence people's attitudes and actions. Before behaviour is put down to individual or group cussedness, managers should look for its possible organizational causes.

Part III

Contrasts in Management

In Part Three we shall look at some of the contrasts in the manager's job. We shall see how greatly it varies according to the situations of the company and the prevailing codes of behaviour. The first chapter describes how the time and the place affect the ways in which a manager thinks and acts. A Japanese or a French manager will often take different decisions from a British manager in the same position. The British manager today will manage differently from his predecessor 100 years ago. The second chapter discusses some of the problems inherent in managing a large organization. The third chapter looks at the ways in which rapid change can revolutionize the nature of the manager's job, and at how to manage change.

8

The Social Environment
of Management

Many management textbooks are written in abstract terms about what managers do and how they do it, but few are concerned with what managers do in real life, still less with why they do it. Once one begins to look at the 'why' of managers' actions, one finds that many of them are influenced by their particular environment. This is true both of the way in which managers behave to other people and of the type of business decisions that they take. How they treat their workers, their junior staff, each other, their directors and their customers, will partly depend on their character, but still more on what is customary at the time in their company, industry, locality, and country. Whether they seek to expand their business rapidly, to undercut their competitors, to misrepresent their products, or to put customer satisfaction before economic production will again, at least partly, depend on the prevailing mores. Social climate comprises all the social factors that affect the way people behave. In this chapter we discuss some of those social factors.

National Differences

What managers strive for, and the rules they observe in doing so, will be influenced, and often determined, by the accepted goals and mores of their society. All managements in private enterprise must be interested in profits, if they are to survive in normal circumstances. The importance they attach to them and how they seek to achieve them will vary in different societies and at different stages in the same society. Economic goals, such as maximum profits, an expanding share of the market, greater productivity and lower costs, will be modified by social goals, such as offering an assured livelihood to long-term employees, even if this means retaining the inefficient, or not causing economic hardship by forcing one's competitor out of business.

In a rapidly industrializing society, managers, whether in private or public industry, are the path-makers who will change or destroy many of the old ways of life. Yet the extent to which business determines the goals of a society varies greatly from one industrial country to another. Perhaps only in America could the head of a nation say, 'The Business of America is Business'.[1] In terms of a country's livelihood this is truer of the UK, but business is still not the core of British society, nor are businessmen the major influence in setting the society's goals. One test of whether business mores dominate society might be whether the explanation of an action as 'good business' is considered more acceptable in the USA than in the UK and more acceptable in the UK than in France. Many common business practices in the UK, such as attempts to mislead the consumer into thinking that a pack is larger or a guarantee more valuable than it is, would be called dishonest by the man in the street.

Visitors and researchers have commented on the differences between American, British, German, French, Russian and Japanese managers, to mention only a few. In Britain continuing concern about our relatively low productivity has led to the search for useful lessons from abroad. A major attempt was made after the Second World War to find out what lessons the USA could teach British industry. British teams of managers, trade unionists and technicians visited the same industries in the USA, under the auspices of the Anglo-American Productivity Council. They enthused about the

---

1. President Coolidge, in a message to the nation, 1924.

atmosphere of American business: the greater optimism, cost consciousness and continual search for improved methods.[2] Americans at all levels are, they reported, more productivity-minded. Previous foreign observers had said the same thing. British visitors to the USA still notice a marked difference today.

The British productivity teams, impressed by the greater American concern for productivity, sought for explanations of this difference in attitude. They found them in the greater social and geographical mobility of American society; the higher status of the businessman and the greater support given to the making of profits and the accumulation of capital; the greater competitiveness, both between companies and individuals; and the more practical, technical orientation of American education. They also pointed to the widespread desire for a higher standard of living and the part played in this by the American woman:

> In this competition for a higher standard of life it is undoubtedly the American woman who is the pacemaker.
>
> In the striving for higher wages, based on higher productivity, the American worker has unquestionably well 'prepared himself unto the battle', and the trumpet sounded by his wife, and to which his unflagging efforts are often the valiant response, does not give 'an uncertain sound' . . . viewed from the standpoint of high national industrial productivity, the influence, in this way, of the American woman must be regarded as distinctly valuable.[3]

Thirty-five years later another British team reported on their visit to the USA to study 'New technology: Manpower aspects of the management of change.' They came from the heavy electrical machinery industry. Like their predecessors they thought that there was a more positive attitude to improvement in the American firms that they visited. Talking about the introduction of new technology in their industry, particularly programmable automation, they said:

2. For a general description of the reports of these teams, see Hutton, Graham, *We Too Can Prosper: The Promise of Productivity*, Allen and Unwin, London, 1953.

3. Anglo-American Productivity Council, 'Internal Combustion Engines', *Productivity Team Report*, p. 7, 1949.

The reason the UK might fall behind could be one of commitment. The American companies met by the Study Group were very motivated to the principle of introducing change rapidly and in a controlled manner. This commitment to the 'management of change' came from the most senior levels and was developed throughout the companies. But that commitment was seen as only the beginning of a series of complex managerial decisions and organisational and motivational adjustments within the company. These changes might more easily be made by North American than by UK companies.[4]

The status of American managers is higher than that of their European counterparts. This has important repercussions, both on recruitment and on the attitudes of top managers. In societies where social prestige is determined by social origins and occupation rather than by one's standard of living, the drawing power of industry's high salaries will be less. British business as a career has suffered, until recently, from the greater prestige of the civil service and the professions, but now business, or at least big business, is becoming more respectable. If successful businessmen have a high status in their society, they will probably be content to devote their energies to business. In a society like the British, where greater prestige still attaches to other occupations, the ambitious and successful businessman who wants a title is likely to devote an increasing amount of time to public activities.

Competition, both between companies and individuals, varies considerably from one country to another. In part this is a result of external pressures. In the USA companies are often forced by anti-trust laws to be more competitive than they would choose. In part the amount of competition depends upon business mores and the ruthlessness with which a company will seek to expand its share of the market.

The amount of competition between individuals and the degree to which inefficiency is tolerated are also strongly

4. Heavy Electrical EDC, Report of the Study Group visit to North America, *New Technology: Manpower Aspects of the Management of Change*, p. 2, National Economic Development Office, London, November 1984.

influenced by the kind of society in which industry grows up. Competition between individuals is stronger in the USA than in Britain. In the USA the inefficient manager will be fired more readily than in Britain. In the latter incompetent but long-service managers in a large company used to be kicked upstairs and given jobs with a high-sounding title but which did not let them handicap the firm's efficiency. Recently they are more likely to have been given generous terms for early retirement. Their livelihood and their feelings would have been spared. In Japan, where the preservation of individual status and prestige is much more important than with us, this practice is the customary one.[5] Promotion is largely by seniority at all levels. The incompetent executive is also spared any loss of face by the acceptance of group responsibility for all decisions.

The recovery of German industry after the war added another country that could be studied to try and discover the reasons for its greater industrial efficiency. The Anglo-German Foundation for the Study of Industrial Society, established in 1973, sponsored a variety of these studies. A major lesson drawn was that the German top manager was much more likely to be an engineer than the British top manager. This finding was probably the reason for the British government providing extra money for ten universities to start joint degrees in engineering and management studies. German managers, perhaps because of their professional background, are more interested in the product than their British counterparts. Peter Lawrence, who has done a number of studies of German managers, points out that: 'Anyone dealing with West Germany should know that his or her counterparts are probably operating on a more technical and specialist model and are product-centred rather than profit-centred.'[6]

Times have changed, and Japan rather than America is now the model for productive enterprise. Both the British

5. Abegglen, James C., *Management and the Worker, The Japanese Solution*, Sophia University in cooperation with Kodansha International, Tokyo, 1973.

6. Lawrence, Peter, *Management in Action*, p. 34, Routledge and Kegan Paul, London, 1984.

and the Americans seek to find out how the Japanese achieve their success. The fear was that the explanation lay in Japanese culture, so that there were no applicable lessons for the West. Fortunately the establishment of Japanese subsidiaries abroad provided an opportunity to study how they managed the locals. In Britain Michael White and Malcolm Trevor found that there were useful if rather shaming lessons for British managers. They found that British workers in Japanese manufacturing companies in this county liked working for Japanese managers and regretted their departure. They liked their greater involvement in production and their more egalitarian approach, compared with British managers. The authors contrast the human relations approach originating in the USA, with its emphasis on the need for managers to be people-centred as well as task-centred, with the Japanese approach, saying:

> . . . Leadership and motivation are subjects which Japanese managers whom we met in Britain hardly talked about. It is true that they set much store by the recruitment of 'good workers', and they took pride in the quality of their workforce. But they seemed to assume that workers would be well motivated. Moreover, to a most striking and extreme degree, they were task-centred in their management style and practices . . . the single-minded Japanese emphasis on the task seems to find a ready acceptance among British workers.[7]

They conclude that:

> One implication is that motivation and leadership are much less a matter of the individual manager's approach and much more a matter of the whole system of working.[8]

The Background of Management

What managers think and how they behave are partly determined by their environment, the country, the stage of

7. White, Michael and Trevor, Malcolm, *Under Japanese Management: The Experience of British Workers*, p. 138, Policy Studies Institute, Heinemann, London, 1983.

8. ibid., p. 139.

industrialization, the locality, and the industry. They are also influenced by their own background, which is in itself a product of their environment. The social and educational background of managers, and the experience they obtain, will depend upon a variety of social and historical facts, such as how industry started in their country, the stage of industrialization, the status of industry in society, the importance attached to different occupations, and the nature and strength of the barriers to occupational mobility. The backgrounds of the early owners and managers differed from one country to another.

Where the family played an important part in the growth of business and still holds many of the top jobs, this may make for conservatism. But family management is not necessarily conservative, as the history of some of the British and German industrial families shows. In many countries family connections are important for getting into management posts. Hence, the power of the family in business can largely prevent management or, at least, top management from being a career open to the talents. In most countries family management has been largely replaced by professional management, though the extent to which this is true varies for historical and taxation reasons.

The professional background of top managers is likely to affect their judgement of what is important: hence company policy. In those countries where engineers predominate, they will probably emphasize production and pay less attention to marketing. Where, as in many large British companies, accountants play an important part in top management, they may be chiefly concerned with the financial standing of the firm, since this affects the ease with which the company can raise capital. The proportion of university graduates among the managers may also affect the attitude to management. The UK is noteworthy for having a smaller proportion of graduates in management than any other Western country except Ireland.

Where graduates are recruited, the jobs they will actually be able to do will be restricted by the strength of local traditions and the extent to which graduates and workers share a common background. It is much more common for

graduates to work as foremen in American than in British
industry. This is partly due to the greater number of college
graduates in the USA, and partly to the greater possibility of
graduates and workers being able to talk the same language.
The American graduate is more likely to have gone to the
same school and to have spent university vacations working
as an operative. In Japan, according to Abegglen, the gulf of
understanding can be too wide to bridge:

> The role of tradition, superstition, and local custom in the actual
> mining operations is very great, and the men can be effectively
> supervised only by foremen and leaders thoroughly familiar with
> these customs and traditions . . . For example if a miner should
> break a dish at breakfast he will under no circumstances go into
> the mine that day, believing that to do so would be certain death.
> Locally trained supervisors understand and respect the belief;
> young graduates of Tokyo's giant universities are less likely to be
> sympathetic. To make the personnel procedures fit the realities
> of supervisory demands in the mine, the company has developed
> a system of having two persons fill each of the intermediate
> supervisory posts. One is an experienced man with years in the
> locality. The other is a young engineer who may or may not
> remain in the local work situation for his full career. He must at
> any rate leave the actual supervision of the miners to his partner.
>   There are many similar situations in Japan; this is merely an
> extreme example of a common problem. The company is caught
> between the quite theoretical training of the Japanese university
> and the social demands of recruitment in the Japanese factory
> which prevent the staffing of managerial posts from the ranks of
> the work force.[9]

In his later book, published in 1973, Abegglen stresses the
durability of Japan's approach to industrial organization.[10]

As industry becomes larger and more complex, the demands
on management become greater. Hence, with increasing
industrialization, the background of managers tends to
change. Professional management, selected and promoted on

9. Abegglen, James, *The Japanese Factory: Aspects of its Social Organization*,
The Free Press, 1958.
10. Abegglen, *Management and the Worker*, op. cit., pp. 191–2.

merit, takes the place of managers chosen by nepotism and the 'old boy' network. This is only true in countries where the class barriers are sufficiently fluid to permit it. Studies in the USA and the UK show that merit is by no means the only qualification for getting to the top. This was true in the 1950s in the UK when the Acton Trust Society studied the background of over 3,000 British managers. This showed that a man who had been to a public school had ten times the average chance of becoming a manager.[11] Comparisons with a study of managers' backgrounds in the USA suggested that the proportion of top managers who came up from the bottom in Britain was 15 per cent and in the USA 20 per cent.[12] 'Up from the bottom' was defined as their having no special educational qualifications, and starting their career as labourers, clerks or salesmen.

A recent large-scale study of British managers analysed the father's occupation for 1,058 members of the British Institute of Management and concluded that:

> . . . a majority of managers came from middle class origins (irrespective of the definition of middle class employed); only just over a quarter originated from the highest echelons of the socio-economic structure as measured by the Registrar General's Class 1 grading. Thus, while modern managers are clearly disproportionately recruited from the upper strata of society, the pattern reveals that origins are not typically exclusive and in no way warrant any suggestion that they constitute a self-perpetuating elite. Indeed, nearly a third of the sample were nurtured in 'blue collar' homes, while the fathers of nearly six per cent were unskilled manual workers.[13]

It is not possible to say whether the social background of British managers has changed over the years because the two

11. The Acton Trust Society, *Management Succession*, op. cit., p. 8.

12. Stewart, Rosemary G. and Duncan-Jones, Paul, 'Educational Background and Career History of British Managers, with some American Comparisons', *Explorations in Entrepreneurial History*, Vol. IX, No. 2, pp. 61–71, December 1956.

13. Poole, Michael, Mansfield, Roger, Blyton, Paul and Frost, Paul, *Managers in Focus: The British Manager in the Early 1980s*, p. 42, Gower, Aldershot, 1981.

samples are not comparable and the methods used for assessing social advantage are different. The later study is based on father's occupation at the height of his career and the former on education and starting job in the company. It is clear that it remains an advantage to have a higher social background if one is to become a manager: an advantage but not a prerequisite.

Management's Attitude to Labour

How managers regard their employees is reflected in management's attitude to authority, on the one hand, and the conditions of work and employee services, on the other. Management's attitude to labour has changed greatly in the last fifty years in Britain and the USA. It also differs considerably from one country to another, and even, to a lesser extent, from one industry or locality to another. Management may be authoritarian (expecting unquestioning obedience to orders and without concern for the employee's welfare); authoritarian and paternalistic; constitutional (acting in accordance with the rules laid down by government, trade unions, and management); or, at least to some extent, democratic (that is, permitting employees some share in decision-making).

How much authority management has and how it exercises it depend partly on the width of the gap that exists in class and education between management and workers, and partly on the limitations on management's freedom of action that are imposed by government and trade unions. Managers' authority generally declines with increasing industrialization. The standard of living rises, making the background of managers and managed more alike, so that management's authority can rest less on social distance.[14]

The gap, or social distance, that exists between different

14. 'Social distance' is the term used by sociologists to describe the extent to which individuals or groups willingly consent to share certain experiences. The smaller the social distance, the more willing they are to share intimate experiences. Sociologists have measured the amount of social distance between different groups by asking people whether they would admit a particular group to close kinship by marriage, to being neighbours in the same street, etc.

levels in the organization reflects both the class structure in the society as a whole and management's place in it. In a very class-bound society much of management's authority may rest on social distance; whether it does so effectively will depend upon the relations existing between management and labour. In a country that still retains some feudal traditions managment may receive the natural social deference that social inferiors give to their superiors. Where no feudal tradition remains, this type of authority is likely to be strongly resented.

Nowadays the part played by government in establishing rules for employee conditions is likely to be the greatest in the early stages of industrialism. Conditions in the older industrial countries set a standard by which employee treatment in the underdeveloped country can be judged, but the unions are not yet powerful enough to ensure adequate protection. So the workers turn to the government. In Latin America the government plays a very active role in industrial relations, partly because of the hesitations that workers, in a highly stratified society, experience in expressing their difficulties direct to management. In such a society there is a much stronger emphasis on authority and deference to the superior than in the English-speaking countries. The workers, therefore, find it easier to get somebody in a government labour department to express their grievances to management.

It should be remembered what a change there has been in Britain, as in other Western countries, in the employer's attitude to the employee. In the early days of industrialization the large majority of British employers, who might otherwise have been kind-hearted men, had no feeling of responsibility for the welfare of their employees and were only forced by the Factory Acts to provide minimal conditions for health and safety. As Croome and Hammond point out:

The new manufacturers, with a few honourable exceptions, felt no responsibility for the welfare of their workers; nor was their own self-interest enlightened enough to show them that better work can be got from well-paid, well-fed, well-housed men and women working under decent conditions for reasonable hours, than from half-starved, brutalized and exhausted workers and over-driven children. The treatment of children in the new factories was, indeed, the crowning disgrace of the Industrial Revolution. Hours in the cotton factories were anything up to sixteen a day and rarely below twelve . . . The workers were completely under the thumb of their 'masters and proprietors', to use the then Lord Londonderry's phrase, subject to arbitrary overtime, arbitrary punishment, arbitrary fines and deductions, and arbitrary dismissal.[15]

Even the differences in some companies between the thirties and the present day are marked. What would be considered normal practice then would be considered inhuman today.

Once management accepts some responsibility for its employees, it may show this in several ways. It may be paternalistic, either because this is, as in Japan, a carry-over from a feudal society, or because management chooses to express its concern for its employees' welfare in that way and meets little or no opposition from them to the dependent role implicit in paternalism. Paternalistic employers are still found in the USA and UK, although they are common in countries like Italy, where class divisions are stronger and where there may still be a master–servant, father–son relation in some companies.

Nor does paternalism necessarily vanish with advancing industrialism, for in Japan, a highly industrialized country, workers are hired for life and almost never sacked.[16] There paternalism even extends to the pay packet, which is based on a variety of factors, of which the most important are the employee's educational status on entering the company and length of service – a system of payment that obviously discourages mobility. The employee will also get a family allowance. Only a small part of the total pay will depend on the kind of work done and on the way it is done.[17] The

15. Croome, H. M. and Hammond, R. J., *An Economic History of Britain*, revised edition, pp. 159–60, Christophers, London, 1947.
16. Abegglen, *Management and the Worker*, op. cit., p. 24.
17. ibid., p. 24.

employee will receive a great range of social benefits from the company for, according to James Abegglen:

> The company is held to be and considers itself responsible for the total person, including his food, clothing, and shelter, and takes a direct responsibility for providing these things along with such items as medical care and education.[18]

Tadashi Hanomi, writing more than twenty years later, similarly describes the 'lifetime welfare system'.[19]

The amount of paternalism will be affected by the extent to which the state provides welfare services. State provision makes the worker, and the manager, less dependent upon a paternalistic employer. Increasingly, good employee conditions in many countries are more of a right than a favour – a right that comes from legislation or from trade union agreements.

Paternalistic management is likely to take what Fox has called a 'unitary' perspective.[20] So do many managers who work for companies where employee rights and conditions are negotiated. The 'unitary' view emphasises the sense of togetherness, the achievement of common organizational goals and the legitimacy of management. Industrial relations problems are seen as either the fault of trade unions or as coming from poor communication and other managerial failings. The opposite perspective Fox called 'pluralist'. This view recognizes that any organization is made up of a variety of interest groups, with management and labour being the two principal ones. Trade unions represent the legitimate interest of labour, and differences with management should be resolved, where possible, by bargaining and compromise. The role of industrial relations is, then, to reach mutually agreed solutions to clashes of interest. Fox made a sharp distinction between the two perspectives. Doing so is always

18. Abegglen, *The Japanese Factory*, op. cit., p. 61.

19. Hanomi, Tadashi, *Labor Relations in Japan Today*, John Martin, London, 1980.

20. Fox, Alan, *Industrial Sociology and Industrial Relations*, Research Paper 3, Royal Commission on Trade Unions and Employers' Associations, HMSO, London, 1966.

a good way of helping people to become conscious of the assumptions that they make: the typical managerial assumption is of a unity of interests. However, the approach of management to employee relations is more varied today than this distinction would suggest.

Five different types of approach to managing industrial relations are suggested by Purcell and Sisson.[21] They call these ideal rather than actual types. These are useful for highlighting different managerial approaches and for helping managers to recognize what approach is used in their own organization. The first is called 'traditionalist', in which management forcefully opposes trade unions and often overtly exploits the employees. The image is of the nineteenth-century capitalist entrepreneur, although the attitude still exists in places. The second is the 'sophisticated paternalist', exemplified by IBM, Hewlett-Packard, Kodak and Marks and Spencer. Purcell and Sisson comment:

> The sophisticated paternalists do not take it for granted that their employees accept the company's objectives or automatically legitimise management decision-making; they spend considerable time and resources in ensuring that their employees have the right approach. Recruitment, selection, training, counselling, high pay and fringe benefits – these and other personal policies are used to ensure that individual aspirations are mostly satisfied, that collective action is seen as unnecessary and inappropriate.[22]

The third type covers the 'sophisticated moderns', who recognize that union participation in some aspects of joint decision-making has advantages for management: for instance, in promoting consent and the handling of change. The authors divide the 'sophisticated moderns' into two groups, which they call 'constitutionalists' and 'consultors'. The former are much more common in the

21. Purcell, John and Sisson, Keith, 'Strategies and Practice in the Management of Industrial Relations', in Bain, George Sayers, *Industrial Relations in Britain*, Blackwell, Oxford, 1983.
22. ibid., p. 114.

USA than in the UK and are based on the idea that, outside collective agreements, management is free to take its own decisions. The latter include companies like ICI and most of the large oil companies. These do not want to codify everything in a collective agreement. Their emphasis is on solving problems rather than on settling disputes. Procedures for consultation are 'usually extremely detailed and wide-ranging, and individual managers will receive considerable training in communications and interpersonal skills'.[23]

Both the sophisticated paternalists and the sophisticated moderns have a fairly uniform approach throughout the organization, and one that has continued for many years. Individual managers are expected to conform to the company's general approach. This contrasts with the last group, the 'standard moderns', which are pragmatic or oppor-tunistic. The examples given are the General Electric Company in the UK, Guest, Keen and Nettlefolds and Tube Investments. Trade unions are recognized, but unlike the other two groups there does not seem to be a common set of values. Hence managers differ in their approach to industrial relations.

Purcell and Sisson explain the differences in approach as primarily due to the attitudes of key personalities at an early stage in the company's development. In the pragmatic 'standard modern' companies the authors could not identify such personalities in the early stages.

How is management likely to exercise authority in the future? There seems little to suggest that many companies will practise effective participative management, which requires both a belief that it is right to do so (which is uncommon among managers and not markedly on the increase) as well as personalities that can cope with the problems inherent in any genuine attempt to encourage employees to share in some aspects of decision-making. Participative management will not work well just because it is law or because management thinks it will pay. Managers who do not genuinely believe that people have a right to share in decisions affecting them

23. ibid., p. 115.

are likely to be irritated by the difficulties that arise in discussions.

In exercising authority managers take many things for granted. A British manager, for instance, used to a society with a long industrial history, will take for granted a work-force that is adapted to industry: that is, one which expects to work regularly and to take orders about the methods and pace of work. Technology has increasingly reduced the opportunities for individuals to behave differently from each other at work, as specialized production requires that people work in a prescribed manner and therefore be subject to external, rather than internal, discipline. British managers who go to an underdeveloped country find that employees are used to an agricultural society, which has a different rhythm of work from an industrial society. It is one that gives labour-ers far more control over the way in which, and the pace at which, they work. Hence the assumptions that managers use to guide them in Britain will no longer be valid. This may cause less difficulty in underdeveloped countries than in other industrial countries, such as France or Italy, where the differ-ences are smaller but may be more difficult to spot. Countries like Nigeria or Peru are so obviously different from Britain that managers may expect differences in employees' attitudes and be prepared to rethink some aspects of their relations with employees. Because the relation between management and worker varies in different countries, most companies operating in other industrial countries try, if they can, to recruit local management to deal with labour.

Labour's Attitude to Management

The way in which management exercises its authority, and the social structure within which it does so, will largely determine labour's view of management. For instance, the attitude of the Japanese workers to their manager will be quite different from that of the British or American.

The extent of national differences in workers' attitudes to management can be illustrated by a study of workers' atti-tudes in four oil refineries belonging to the same company in France and Britain. This study found that the former took a much more critical view of management than did the latter.[24] The British were found to be broadly content with their incomes and standard of living, while the French were dissatisfied. They resented their situation as manual workers in French society. They were also 'deeply convinced that the principles determining salary allocation within the industry were unfair; the British, on the other hand were overwhelmingly satisfied with them'.[25] The French workers were much more militant about shift working and manning. The criticisms that the French and British workers made of management also differed. The main French criticism was of the high degree of social distance that existed between management and workers. 'Management was seen as aloof and cold, fundamentally uninterested in the workers as human beings.' The British criticisms were primarily technical ones of management's efficiency, though these were not accompanied by a demand for more control by the workers. The British workers saw management as working in the interests of everyone, while the French workers saw management as exploitive, being primarily concerned with the shareholders' interests. This was illustrated by their attitudes to power and control, as Gallie says:

> The French felt that the existing structure of power was illegitimate, and a clear majority would have been prepared to see an extension of worker control over management's powers of decision into the very heart of the traditional areas of managerial prerogative, including the most fundamental strategic decisions about financial budgeting and new investment. In contrast, the British workers showed a high level of contentment with the existing procedures of decision making.

Gallie suggests that the difference in attitudes may be partly explained by the fact that the French managers remained sovereign at the refinery, while in the British refineries the shop-floor representatives have control, in the sense of a power of veto, over many aspects of work organization.

24. Gallie, Duncan, *In Search of the New Working Class: Automation and Social Integration within the Capitalist Enterprise*, Cambridge University Press, Cambridge, 1978.
25. ibid., p. 296.

Labour's attitudes to management differ in different countries. There are also industrial differences that at least partially cut across national boundaries, as strike figures show. Many people, including managers in strike-free companies, say that managers get the labour relations they deserve. This is only a half-truth, for it is much harder to have good industrial relations in some industries than in others. A good management may be handicapped by a legacy of bad relations in the company, which may take years to live down, or by being in an industry with a long record of bad relations.

Analysis of strike figures shows that some industries have a much higher incidence of strikes than others, and that this is true for the same industries in many different countries. A study of man–days lost through strikes over a number of years in eleven countries showed that, with an occasional exception, it was possible to discern a similar pattern of incidence of strikes.[26] The authors of the study attribute the differences in the propensity to strike to social reasons.

The main reason, they think, why miners and dockers in all countries have such a high propensity for striking is that they are an isolated, relatively homogeneous mass, almost a race apart, living in their own communities with their own distinctive ways of life. They share the same grievances, do similar work and have similar experiences. It is also hard to get out of this mass; the skills are specialized and not transferable. The opportunities for promotion are also limited. According to Kerr and Siegel: 'The strike for this isolated mass is a kind of colonial revolt against far-removed authority, an outlet for accumulated tensions, and a substitute for occupational and social mobility.'[27] There are two other reasons they suggest for an industry to be especially strike-prone: that the group is capable of uniting, which generally results from close, continuous contact; and that the work is unpleasant and thus provides plenty of opportunities for grievances.

26. Kerr, Clark and Siegel, Abraham, 'The Interindustry Propensity to Strike – an International Comparison', in *Industrial Conflict* (edited by Kornhauser, A., Dubin, R. and Ross, A. M.), McGraw-Hill, New York, 1954.
27. ibid., p. 193.

More recent figures for the UK also show a continued wide disparity in stoppages between industries. The figures in Table 8.1 show the annual average from 1966 to 1973 for some of the industries with high and low figures.[28]

TABLE 8.1

	No. of working days lost per 1,000 employees
Distributive trades	6.5
Leather, leather goods and fur	17.6
Clothing and footwear	90.1
Chemical and allied industries	136.8
Shipbuilding and marine engineering	1,820.4
Vehicles	2,105.3
Mining and quarrying	4,305.5

This short account of industrial differences in the likelihood of strikes is one illustration of the way in which differences in social structure can affect management problems. It may perhaps make managers in relatively strike-free industries more sympathetic with the trials of their colleagues in less favourably placed industries.

SUMMARY

Why managers think and act as they do depends partly on the type of people they are, but more on their environment. This is made up of the social and economic history of the country in which they are working, including the stage of industrialization; the position of business in society; the prevailing moral standards; the relation of the social classes; the strength of the trade union movement; and the number and type of government regulations. Both the methods of conducting

28. 'The Incidence of Industrial Stoppages in the United Kingdom', p. 115, *Department of Employment Gazette*, Feb. 1976.

business and the attitudes to employees will mainly depend on what is customary at that time and place.

The educational and social background of managers varies in different countries. This is one reason why the approach of the French businessman tends to be different from that of the British, and both of them different from the Japanese. In some countries the family still plays a dominant role, although its influence is now small in the US and the UK. Even so, in both countries managers' social background still has a considerable influence on their chances of becoming a manager. The professional background of a manager can also influence his or her view of management. In Germany, where engineers play a big role in management, the approach to business is likely to be different from Britain, where accountants are more favoured for top management. The Japanese are more task-oriented than the British and more egalitarian in their relations with workers.

How management exercises authority differs over time, as well as between countries. One factor influencing it is the width of the social gap that exists between management and workers. In some countries managers still receive a feudal deference from their workers. With increasing industrialization management's authority declines, partly because a rising standard of living reduces the distance between management and workers, partly because trade unions and government regulations restrict management's freedom of action. Five different approaches to industrial relations today were described. Most stem from the values held by a key figure in company history.

Labour's attitude to management is a response to how management treats the workers. It is also a reflection of the social structure. This was illustrated by the very different attitudes to management of British and French workers in oil refineries owned by the same company. There are marked differences between industries as well as between countries, and in the same country at different periods in its history. Some industries, for instance, have been shown to be strike-prone. Hence, it is only partly true to say that management gets the labour relations it deserves.

9

Management in Large Organizations

What difference does size make to the problems of managing people and getting organizations to work effectively? This is the question that we shall address in this chapter. It is an important one because large organizations form a substantial part of the economy. Some management problems become more difficult in large organizations, others become easier, while yet others are a mixture of the two. We shall briefly review the advantages, then concentrate on the disadvantages in the belief that a clearer awareness of what they are, and of what may be done to lessen them, is needed.

The Advantages of Large Organizations

The main financial and technical advantages of large companies – the reasons for many mergers and take-overs – are the following: the economics of large-scale production; easier access to finance; the spread of risks, including better opportunities for diversification; and the ability to undertake very expensive technical tasks. The last can be a key reason for mergers in industries that have a heavy expenditure on research and development. Another advantage is that a large company is more powerful and, therefore, less likely to be taken over. Even so, size does not guarantee protection, as many large companies have found.

One of the most important advantages of a large firm, according to Edwards and Townsend, is that its size enables exceptional managerial abilities to be used to the full.[1] There is, however, the corresponding disadvantage that managers with exceptional abilities are scarce, and a large organization that does not have outstanding managers may run into difficulties. Its managers might be completely satisfactory in a smaller company but not be able to cope successfully with the scale of problems in a large organization. It is one's estimate of the supply of exceptional managerial ability that will determine whether one agrees with Edwards' and Townsend's arguments. Certainly, the anxiety shown by some of the most successful large companies about how to get good top managers suggests that the supply is too small to meet the demand. Occasionally outstanding managers are found in medium-sized companies, where their abilities may be restricted by lack of capital. Then a merger with a larger company can give them greater scope.

The large firm usually has an advantage in recruiting staff, especially for management posts. Many people prefer to be associated with a large, well-known company for its reputation (outside people will have heard of the company where they work), for its better facilities, greater security (less true than it used to be) and better opportunities for promotion to interesting and well-paid jobs. The large company is also able to spend more time and money on trying to attract the people it wants. It will have an advantage in promotion, too, because it will have a bigger pool on which to draw, particularly for management posts. Although the big company has an advantage in recruitment, there are people at all levels who will prefer to work for a small or medium-sized one.

The Disadvantages of Large Organizations

The greatest problem of large-scale organization is how to prevent feelings of indifference or frustration. Junior and middle management may feel frustrated because they are a

1. Edwards and Townsend, *Business Enterprise: Its Growth and Organization*, op. cit., p. 183.

long way from effective authority. Workers, both manual and clerical, may feel little or no identification with the company where they work. All may miss the feeling of personal loyalty and commitment that can come from working for 'the boss'. Even the chief executive may feel frustrated because of the number of people who may need to be consulted before an important decision is taken.

It is lower down the management hierarchy that feelings of frustration are most likely. These may be caused by long delays in getting a decision, by poor communication with related departments, and by uncertainties about the scope of the person's authority. Two features of large-scale organization can be the sources of many of the difficulties: a long chain of command and a large number of specialists. The length of the chain will depend upon the pattern of organization. If it is a 'flat' one, where a large number of managers report to one person, there may be only three links in the chain on the sales side and four or five on production; but in large organizations, modelled on the span of control theory, there may be as many as twelve or more. Each additional level in the management hierarchy is a potential obstacle to communication. Each reduces the responsibility of those below, so that those at the bottom of the management ladder, or even part of the way up, may feel frustrated by the small opportunity for exercising responsibility. How serious this feeling is likely to be will depend on the extent of centralization, and on the consistency and clarity of the policies for what decisions can be taken at different levels.

A long chain of command and a large number of specialists make managers' jobs highly specialized ones compared to their counterpart in a small, or medium-sized, undertaking. Hence it is harder for them to get experience of different functions, or to have much conception of the business as a whole. So long as they remain in middle management, this may not matter, but those who are promoted to top management will need a wider experience and knowledge. The difficulties of producing general managers in an organization where all, except those right at the top, are specialists is one of the problems of large organizations, although a policy of wide rotation can do much to avoid it. Some top managers of large companies bewail the absence of small subsidiaries, where they could give their bright young people some experience of general management. Another, related, difficulty is that some of those who might make good top managers are not prepared for the long slog in positions of little responsiblity which is a prerequisite for promotion in many large companies, especially in those with a many-tiered hierarchy. Hence some keen young people will opt for smaller companies, where they can make a mark more quickly and get a wide experience of management, which will be useful later if they want to move.

A feeling among junior and lower-middle managers that they are far removed from effective authority is one of the dangers of large organizations. This feeling can be more pronounced on the shop floor, which may be faced with a local management that does not have the authority to give a decision on a question raised by the union or by the workers' representatives on the joint consultative committee.

The most frequently mentioned problem of large organizations is not the frustrations of lower management but the difficulties of creating or maintaining good management–worker relations. The interest in incentives, and in ways of encouraging greater management–worker cooperation, all stem from the divorce between the two, which can develop as a firm grows larger. In the smallest firm, such as a small builder and decorator, the workers may identify themselves with the business. As it grows from 5 employees to 50, from 50 to 100 and from 100 to 500, there will be changes in the relation between the boss and employees, even if 'the boss' remains the same. Above about 600 employees no manager can really know all the employees; hence that form of personal knowledge comes to an end. Employees' feelings of personal responsibility for the success of the company diminish as the company grows: whether they are late or absent becomes a purely personal question that may be affected by penalties for bad timekeeping rather than by a concern for any disruption they may cause.

The size of the organization may, depending upon the way in which it is organized and how it has grown, have an important effect on the morale of the junior and middle managers. The size of the establishment, that is, the individual producing unit, whether factory, colliery, power station, retail store or hospital, is more important in its effects on workers' morale than the size of the company as a whole. The importance of size of establishment has been shown by studies over the years. The first in 1953 tried to assess workers' morale – the level of enthusiasm for work – by comparing the amount of time people took off work.[2] The assumption made was that if people's morale was high, they would take less time off work than if it was low. The study compared the lost-time rates in different sized establishments: in the coal industry, in a large retail chain-store, and in a manufacturing company. In all three absenteeism was higher in the larger units.

The relation between absenteeism and size of establishment was also found in a different form of organization – hospitals. Statistics of 837,000 hospital workers employed in 4,360 American hospitals in 1953 showed a steady increase in the mean accident rate with the size of hospital. The rate, for all accidents causing absence other than on the day of the accident, was more than five times as great in a hospital with over 2,000 workers as it was in a hospital with less than 20.[3] A high rate of absenteeism can be a major problem for management. It was one of the main reasons behind the new forms of smaller, more autonomous, work units introduced in Sweden. A high rate of labour turnover was another reason.[4]

The size-effect on workers' attitudes can also be found in the working group itself. According to Revans, 'it is not only the total size of the coal-mine that influences the willingness of men to cooperate; this willingness is also markedly determined by the average size of the groups within the mine in which men work'.[5] A study made in 1969 in the Dunlop company also found that the size and structure of the

2. Acton Society Trust, *Size and Morale*, The Trust, London, 1953.
3. Revans, R. W., 'Is Work Worthwhile?', *Personnel Management*, Vol. XI, No. 343, pp. 12–21, Institute of Personnel Management, London, March 1958.
4. Gregory, Denis (ed.), *Work Organization: Swedish Experience and British Context*, SSRC, London, 1978.
5. Revans, op. cit.

working group was an important influence upon the amount of absenteeism. The study recommended the establishment, wherever possible, of small, well-defined units so as to promote feelings of loyalty.[6]

The number of industrial disputes also increased with the size of establishment, as is strikingly shown in Table 9.1. This study of industrial disputes in Britain between mid-1979 and mid-1980 concluded that 'there is a strong relationship between the occurrence of every type of industrial action and the number of manual workers at the establishment'.[7] The authors suggest that there is a 'threshold effect', as some forms of industrial action are only possible when a certain number of workers are in a single establishment. The winter of 1979–80 was called 'the winter of discontent' because of the amount of industrial action then.

TABLE 9.1 – Percentage of industrial action by manual workers between mid-1979 and mid-1980 by the number of manual workers in the establishment

	Any type of industrial action %	Strike/ lockout %
Total	18	12
No. of manual workers		
1–9	2	2
10–24	8	5
25–49	13	8
50–99	27	18
100–199	33	21
200–499	50	40
500–999	74	53
1000+	77	67

6. Quoted in Incomes Data Services Study, No. III, December 1975.
7. Daniel, W. W. and Millward, Neil, *Workplace Industrial Relations in Britain*, The DE/PSI/SSRC Survey, p. 218, Heniemann, London, 1983.

So far we have not mentioned what are traditionally supposed to be the disadvantages of large organization: inflexibility, red-tape, and empire-building. Obviously these are all well-known temptations, to judge only by the roar of approval that greeted *Parkinson's Law*.[8] The amount of formal information, whether on paper or discs, must go up as a company grows and artificial eyes and ears have to be substituted for personal knowledge and word of mouth. Both the amount of paper and the rate of empire-building may be increased if managers feel insecure; they may record everything to protect themselves, or build empires to bolster their prestige, and there is always a temptation to add to them. Yet the dangers of red-tape and empire-building in large organizations can be held in check.

More difficult problems are inflexibility and delay. The process of working out the general aims of the organization, getting agreement for changes, keeping each part of the organization informed, and checking it if it departs from the common aims and plan, is a laborious one. There may be so many people to be consulted before an important decision is made that it can take much longer in a large company than in a medium-sized one. As long ago as 1925 Alfred E. Sloan, chairman of General Motors, bemoaned that:

> In practically all our activities we seem to suffer from the inertia resulting from our great size. It seems to be hard for us to get action when it comes to a matter of putting our ideas across. There are so many people involved and it requires such a tremendous effort to put something new into effect, that a new idea is likely to be considered insignificant in comparison with the effort that it takes to put it across.
>
> . . . Sometimes I am almost forced to the conclusion that General Motors is so large that it is impossible for us to really be leaders.[9]

8. Parkinson, C. Northcote, *Parkinson's Law or the Pursuit of Progress*, John Murray, London, 1958.
9. From a speech to General Motors' sales committee, 29 July 1925, quoted by the Temporary National Economic Committee, *Relative Efficiency of Large, Medium-Sized and Small Business*, Monograph 13, pp. 130–1, US Government Printing Office, Washington, 1941.

Nor are the problems of inertia likely to be much different in today's large organizations. All of them have to cope with the fact that the amount of energy required to oppose is much less than that required to initiate and carry through a change. How much inertia and resistance there will be depends partly upon the background and calibre of the people recruited, partly on the atmosphere within the company and partly on how used its managers are to change.

Different Ways of Being Big

So far we have talked about the problems of large-scale organization as if they were common to all large companies. So indeed they are, but their intensity will vary according to how the firm has grown, how it is organized, and what stage it has reached in its history. Organizations can become big in different ways: they can grow gradually, like Shell Petroleum, or with greater rapidity, like Racal Electronics, which increased its turnover from £54 million in 1975 to £816 million in 1984. Large organizations, like ICI, can be created by the amalgamation of a small number of fair-sized companies, or, in exceptional circumstances, they can become big overnight as when 800 companies were changed into the National Coal Board. The difficulties experienced in the early days of the large nationalized industries in the UK were particularly acute because of the huge and sudden increase in the size of the organization. Unhappily, the decades since then provide similar, if less acute, examples of the problems of large organizations, especially those formed by mergers and take-overs. Even the expected economic advantages of such mergers have often proved disappointing.[10]

The rate of growth intensifies management problems of coordination and human relations because tradition can play little or no part. Much of the work of an organization is carried out through informal contact. But in a company created by amalgamation there will be no common 'old-boy' network and its growth will inevitably take time. A lengthy

10. Meeks, G., *Disappointing Marriage: A Study of the Gains from Mergers*, CUP, Cambridge, 1977.

mutual process of getting to know one another, both in terms of recognition and of assessment, will have to go on. In some ways a company that expands very rapidly has fewer problems than one that is created by amalgamations, or grows through mergers, because it will have a core of people who know each other on which to build. In other ways it can be more difficult, because the changes that have to be made may be less obvious than they are in an amalgamation.

Companies may continue to grow by mergers as well as by expansion of existing resources. Any merger creates problems of how to fit the new company into the existing structure. The parent, unless it is only a financial holding company, will seek, to a greater or lesser extent, to mould the new acquisition to the parental pattern. The technical, financial, and administrative changes may amount to almost complete integration or only to control of selected aspects of the business. In theory these changes need not take long but, if the management of the parent organization is anxious not to kill the growing tree in the process, not to destroy management initiative and enthusiasm, they will have to be made slowly. Unless it is a relatively small acquisition, the parent company may also gradually change during the process of adjustment. Hence the necessity, underlined by a number of organizations with experience of mergers, for allowing sufficient time for digestion before embarking on a new merger.

Whatever the difficulties for management created by large-scale organization, they do not prevent many large firms from growing still larger. The financial and technical advantages of size are usually sufficient to outweigh the disadvantages. The share of the 100 largest firms in UK manufacturing net output during the period 1909–70 rose from 15 per cent to 45 per cent.[11] In the recession of the late seventies and early eighties many large organizations were cut back. Others continued to expand, so that the numbers of firms employing over 10,000 remained more or less constant. Since large organizations form a major part of the economy, it is important

11. Hannah, L., *The Rise of the Corporate Economy*, Appendix 2, p. 216, Methuen, London, 1976.

to examine what can be done to reduce their disadvantages, and especially their disadvantages for the employee, whether manager or worker.

What Can Be Done?

The list of disadvantages of large-scale organizations is a long one: a many-tiered management structure, with its dangers of poor communication and a feeling of remoteness from effective authority; junior and middle managers who feel that they do not have enough responsibility; managers who feel their authority is threatened by specialists; specialists who feel frustrated because their advice is not taken; workers who feel their contribution does not matter and who become indifferent to the success of the company; inflexibility, form-filling, and empire-building. Yet even then the list is not exhaustive. These are dangers inherent in large-scale organizations, but they can all be mitigated if not avoided. They are problems that may have to be lived with, but that can be kept in check by awareness and watchfulness. Some problems can even be averted: there are large companies with excellent labour relations.

Much can be done, by the philosophy and policies of management and by changes in the organization structure, to reduce the human disadvantages of bigness. In the list of disadvantages in the previous paragraph the word 'feel' recurs. People in large organizations can more easily feel unimportant, insecure and, if they are managers or foremen, uncertain of their authority or prospects. But it is not inevitable that they should feel like that in a large organization. A management that really believes that people are individuals, and that individuals matter, can constantly seek to give effect to this belief. It may, for instance, experiment with increasing the content of jobs if it thinks that people find their jobs too narrow. It can promote those who share its belief in the importance of individuals.

One of the ways in which the anonymity of top management – with all its possible implications of a lack of feeling – may be lessened, even in the largest organization, is by the actions of the chief executive. If he or she really cares about individuals, and is able to make this public knowledge, it can influence the attitudes of employees at all levels. This was strikingly shown in one company where the managing director not merely cared deeply about the welfare of his employees, but wrote and broadcast about his philosophy of management so that many of his employees had heard of it. He also made a point of visiting any newly acquired company and meeting many of its employees. The result was that a number of the managers in these companies, when interviewed about their reactions to the merger, said that they felt they could go to the managing director if they had a complaint and get a fair deal. Another managing director said that he regarded his appearances on television as one way of being known to his employees.

Much can also be done by the form of the organization to prevent people from feeling frustrated. Companies with small working groups and small establishments will tend to have fewer problems with worker morale and cooperation than those with large establishments and large working groups. The nature of its business will determine what choice a company has in this aspect of its organization, but at least managers should be aware of the importance of any element of choice there may be.

Good human relations requires more conscious thought and effort in a large organization than in a small one, where the right attitude can take a manager much further. In a large organization managers need to understand the possible sources of frustration. They may not see the symptoms of frustration until they show in lost-time rates, high labour turnover, strikes and management ulcers. A manager who remembers, for instance, that a long delay in getting a decision, uncertainty about the scope of one's authority or the views of one's superior can be frustrating will take more trouble to avoid these than an equally well-intentioned manager who does not.

Many problems are intensified in a highly centralized organization which encourages red-tape and resistance to change and which gives the more junior managers little opportunity to exercise responsibility. Therefore, an important organizational aim is to centralize as little as possible and to keep the number of tiers in the management hierarchy to the minimum. But the 'as possible' is important. What is possible will vary at different periods in a company's history. More centralization may be necessary in the early days of a merger than later.

How much decentralization is possible also varies in different industries; the opportunities for it are obviously less in oil refining or in steel making than in industries where production can economically be broken down into separate units. Some companies are inescapably committed to large establishments, which are probably more important factors in morale than the size of the company. Others may have some choice both in the size of their establishments and in whether they divide their company – as so many successful large companies are divided – into semi-autonomous subsidiaries or divisions. If it is possible to judge the profitability of a subsidiary, it is easier to go further in decentralization, as it can then be treated in many ways as a separate economic unit.

The minimum of centralization that is customary in a large organization is financial control over capital expenditure above a stated figure, approval of financial budgets, controls over top level appointments and remuneration, and probably the conduct of national trade union negotiations. There may also be a staff of specialists at headquarters, although many companies now limit their head office to the staff necessary to operate these central controls. According to Edwards and Townsend:

> Provided one decides rightly which types of decisions to allow to come to the centre there is no reason why the problem of coordination should make a large firm less efficient than two or more smaller, independent firms. This does not mean that no large firms will suffer from unwieldiness, woolliness and slowness; but if they do so it will be because of deficiencies in particular managements, not because of the inevitable deficiencies of large organizations. Small firms may equally suffer from deficiencies in management and very frequently do.

There is no stage at which an organization must become less efficient than it would be if it were smaller; but beyond the point where economies of large outputs and cost-reducing advantages of large organizations are exhausted it will not be more efficient.[12]

It is arguable whether good organization – meaning, especially here, the right balance between centralization and decentralization – can overcome all the disadvantages of coordination in large organizations, as Edwards and Townsend claim. The problem of the number of people to be consulted must still remain, as must that of keeping all parts of the organization informed when necessary. That large firms can be efficient and small firms inefficient is clear, but to manage a large company as efficiently as a small one requires a higher calibre of management.

SUMMARY

The continued growth in the number and size of large companies shows that economically their advantages outweigh their disadvantages, though the sceptic may say that the ability of the large fish to swallow the small is no reflection on the efficient functioning of the latter. Despite its economic advantages, a large organization has inherent difficulties, which its managers must combat. To do so successfully requires better managers than in a smaller company. The large company is fortunate in being in a stronger position for recruiting such men and women.

One of the greatest problems of large-scale organization is how to prevent feelings of indifference or frustration. The workers may feel that their contribution does not matter and that nobody cares about them. They will find it hard to identify with the success of the organization. The managers may be frustrated because of delays in getting a decision, or because of poor communication. They may feel that they do not have enough responsibility; in part because of the number of tiers in the management structure, and in part because they may feel plagued by specialists. Promotion is

12. Edwards and Townsend, *Business Enterprise: Its Growth and Organization*, op. cit., p. 195.

usually slower, and it is harder for managers to get experience for top management if middle-management posts are highly specialized.

As an organization grows larger, the gap between management and workers widens. Various studies of the effects of size show that the larger the number employed in an establishment, the lower is morale, as measured by lost-time rates, strikes and accidents. The size of the working group also affects absenteeism.

The traditional temptations of large-scale organization are inflexibility, red-tape, and empire-building. These dangers can be kept in check, although never abolished. But the inertia level of large organizations may always be higher than that of the efficient small company.

Although there are common problems of bigness, they will be more intense in some companies than others. It depends how the company has become big. If it has grown rapidly, whether by amalgamation or natural expansion, its problems will be greater than those of a company that has grown gradually, building on, and developing its tradition as it grows.

It is obvious that some large organizations keep many of these problems under control. Their management philosophy and policies help to prevent people feeling unimportant, insecure, and frustrated. In a few the chief executive's obvious personal concern for the staff can do much to reassure them that 'the boss' does care. The type of organization can also help to prevent a feeling of remoteness; as far as possible, there should be small groups, small establishments, and a decentralized organization. As Dr Schumacher said 'the fundamental task is to achieve smallness within the organization'.[13]

13. Schumacher, E. F., *Small is Beautiful*, p. 202, Abacus, London, 1974.

10

The Manager and Change

This chapter is in two parts. The first describes the major changes affecting management and what can be done to plan for them. The second discusses what has been learnt about how to implement change successfully.[1]

Many of the realities of management change little or are modified gradually, but some are revolutionized. This is true of the extent to which companies, even very large companies, are vulnerable to external changes. The oil crisis was a dramatic example, but there are many others as managers in more and more companies have to seek for their business overseas and to face competition from both the old and the newly industrialized countries. Changes in technology and in government policies have also had a radical impact on managers in many companies and in public service organizations.

One of the most difficult problems for managers is rapid change. How British managers react to change will have an important influence on Britain's economic future. This is true

---

1. The management of change is such an important subject that this is also discussed in the companion volume, *The Reality of Organizations*, where examples of how change was managed successfully in a number of different kinds of organization are given.

for managers in the public service as well as for those in industry and commerce. The tempo of change has speeded up; hence the demands made on managers to plan for, and adjust to, change are greater. All change requires both abilities. Some changes can be planned for in great detail, such as the switch to a new model. Others may be unforeseeable, but if the organization is kept sufficiently flexible, it will be able to cope with the unexpected. The number of completely unexpected changes can be kept to a minimum by foresight. Changes also mean adjustment. Without it the planning will be unsuccessful. Adjustment is usually more difficult for managers than planning, because it has an emotional aspect to it, both for them and for their staff. They have to be able to acclimatize both themselves and their subordinates to the change. The sources of major change affecting management are:

1. Political changes affecting both the public service and industry and commerce.
2. Greater competition both at home and abroad.
3. Innovations, which lead to new products and new methods of working.
4. Changes in consumer expenditure as a result of innovations, of changes in consumer wants and of new methods of selling.
5. Changes in the background, training and occupation of those employed.
6. Spread of industrial action to other occupations and organizations.
7. The growth of information technology.

Let us look at each of these in turn to see what management can do to plan for them.

Changes Affecting Management

Political Changes

The government can affect the work of managers in a number of ways, but most commonly by changing taxation affecting companies and by introducing employment legislation.

It can also make changes that have a more direct impact on a large number of managers' jobs. It can change the structure and ownership of an organization by nationalization and privatization. It can influence the amount of competition by regulating take-overs. It can reorganize public service organizations, as the British Government has the National Health Service and some local authorities. It can change the rules within which different types of businesses have operated for many years, as it has those affecting financial institutions. In Britain in the first half of the eighties the effects of political changes on management were greater than they had been since the nationalization measures of the first post-war Labour government. A radical Conservative government sought to make managers in the public service more aware that they *were* managers, and hence more accountable. It sought to make changes that would improve the efficiency of public services and of private industry. In the Greater London Council, before it was abolished, a radical Labour administration also changed many officers' work by its determination to see its policies implemented, including its support for the employment opportunities of minority groups and of women.

Changes in the amount and type of taxes are usually unpredictable. Some industries are particularly vulnerable to alterations in taxes that affect sales. The adjustments for companies in such industries are bound to be severe, but something can be done to prepare for their possibility. A planned employment policy may be able to provide for some of the labour force in peak periods to consist of part-time married women or retired employees, and a redundancy policy can be agreed with the unions if necessary. Some companies may also seek to mitigate the severity of the adjustments by diversification to products that will not be affected in the same way. Tax changes affecting investment decisions usually provide opportunities for planning in a way that taxes affecting sales do not.

The political changes affecting managers in many organizations have been so great in the early eighties that they merit being listed first amongst the changes affecting British managers, particularly managers in the public services. Managers in many companies are more affected by changes in technology, markets and in the economy.

Some political changes can be anticipated by managers and plans made accordingly. A few may be prevented or modified by lobbying, but, for most, planning is limited to dealing with the consequences.

Greater Competition

The recession of the late seventies and early eighties intensified the competition experienced by managers in the Western world. So did the growth of the Far Eastern economies. This competition was a major reason for the contraction that managers in many manufacturing companies had to carry through. More managers became experienced in managing rundown. The pressure of competition provided the stimulus to managers in many different industries to try and improve the efficiency of their operations. It was also the reason for a greater interest in strategic planning, as more managers realized the need to assess the strengths and weaknesses, threats and opportunities facing their companies. The problems of the European economies in the early eighties also affected the public services, as governments looked for ways of economizing. Managers in all kinds of organizations needed to become better at managing their resources and were more likely than in the past to be penalized if they did not.

Innovations

The tempo of innovation is much greater than before; hence in some industries a company must spend heavily on research and development if it is to survive. To avoid stagnation or decline it must ever be on the look-out for new possibilities for growth. A seminal early study by the Stanford Research Institute[2] of the causes of company growth in the USA

2. The companies studied were those manufacturing companies listed in *Moody's Industrials*, an American company reference book, which from 1939 to 1949 had an increase in sales of at least 400 per cent. The sales history of these companies was also followed from 1949 to 1956. They were compared with companies that had a low rate of sales increase.

showed that the leading areas of growth change within a few years. Hence one of the important problems for management in a rapidly changing industry is to make certain that it is producing the right things and that it does not go on producing them for too long.

Diversification into other industries, and into other parts of the same industry, is one answer to the need to protect the company from a decline in its products. There is a danger, however, that a company may diversify without sufficient study of what products and markets are likely to grow, and of which ones are suitable for the company – suitable in terms of its capital, location, access to raw materials, and managerial know-how. In diversification by merger the latter will be enlarged by the experience of the managers in the other company. This may provide a solution to the problem of inadequate managerial know-how in the new industry, provided the acquiring company can retain the key people.

Innovation is a lengthy business, so the company will have to plan well ahead. In selecting a research project it will have to judge the following: the likelihood of success; the time it will take; and its costs and its value, judged by the likely market gain and by the need for a new or improved product. The latter will mainly depend on the competitive position and the rate of obsolescence of existing products. Completing the research project and deciding to manufacture a new product are only the first stages in launching a new product. Management may be stronger at one stage of the process of innovation than at another. They may, for instance, be better at analysing a problem and reaching a decision than they are at getting sufficient agreement to make the implementation successful. Or they may get into difficulties at the implementation stage because top management considers speed synonymous with efficiency and, therefore, tends to skimp the preliminary stages. The launching of a new product may also come to grief because of the way in which it is marketed. Selling a new product may mean entering a new market and competing against those familiar with it. Curiously, some companies plan the design and manufacture of a new product with great care, but treat the marketing of it as if it was a routine matter, although the market they are entering may need quite different methods from their customary ones. They may also attach too much importance to the goodwill their name has earned elsewhere, but which may have little value in a new market where others are already established. There is also the opposite danger of concentrating too much on the marketing and too little on the timing and quality of production.

The chances of future success would be greater if companies more often analysed the causes of their failure. It is useful to find out at what stage the project ran into difficulties. This may show up a recurrent weakness at a particular stage. Unfortunately management is often chary of analysing the causes of failure, either because it will not face up to the fact of failure or because it is afraid of upsetting people.

Changes in Consumer Expenditure

The pattern of consumer expenditure changes rapidly. The age distribution of the population, the age of marriage, the average number of children and how soon after marriage they are born, the proportion of women working, the level of education, the amount of leisure, and the availability of goods, all have changed in recent years and all influence what consumers buy and when. A major factor determining how money is spent is the standard of living and how it is distributed both between occupations and between age groups. Another is changes in fashions, such as the growth of informality and its effects on what people wear.

The volume of consumer spending in the United Kingdom has fluctuated in recent years, making life more difficult for retailers and some manufacturers of consumer goods. In 1970 total UK consumers' expenditure was £31.7 billion. Correcting to 1970 prices, it rose to £36.0 billion in 1973, and from 1974 to 1977 it was below 1973. It increased sharply in 1978 and 1979 and fell slightly in 1980. It recovered in 1982 to the peak 1979 level.

During the decade from 1972 to 1982 consumers' spending habits changed as they spent more on some goods and less on others. Real spending (that is, adjusted for inflation) on food and fuel grew by 3 and 4 per cent respectively, and on alcohol by 19 per cent, although in 1982 it was 10 per cent below that in 1979. Real expenditure on post and telecoms rose by 73 per cent, on TV and video by 133 per cent, while that on books and newspapers fell by 15 per cent and tobacco by 17 per cent.[3]

The company that correctly foresees future consumer wants can get into a growing market at the beginning. It might take as a general guide that today's affluent consumer is tomorrow's average consumer, although it should check on how many other manufacturers are acting on the same principle.

Changes in the Composition of the Working Force

The management ratio, that is, the proportion of management staff, including specialists, to total employees, varies greatly between companies of the same size. Part of this difference is due to the number of staff employed in research and development. A study of the changing employment structure of fifty American companies since the Second World War shows that the largest increase in the proportion of senior staff took place in the firms that were making the greatest number of changes. The firms that were innovating least showed almost no increase.[4]

At the beginning of the twentieth century the majority of American people lived in rural settlements and made a living from farming. By 1940 this group had been over-taken by industrial, especially semi-skilled, workers. The picture had changed again by 1960 when the largest single group was 'professional, managerial, and technical people'.[5] By the 1980s this group comprised the majority of working

3. *Social Trends*, No. 14, HMSO, 1984.

4. Hill, Samuel E. and Harbison, Frederick, 'Manpower and Innovation in American Industry', Industrial Relations Section, Princeton University, 1959, quoted by Harbison and Myers, op. cit., pp. 26–7.

5. Drucker, Peter F., *The Age of Discontinuity*, p. 248, Heinemann, London, 1969.

172   *The Reality of Management*

Americans. This means that the education, occupation and outlook of the people that managers are working with, whether as subordinates or colleagues, has changed. Drucker highlighted how management is affected, when much of its time is spent managing knowledge workers. He says:

> The position of these people, however, we do not yet fully understand. Nor do we know how to manage them, that is, how to make their knowledge, their efforts, their contribution effective in the performance of the whole. This is a problem which few, if any, of the founding fathers of management could have foreseen, it is a problem that only arose because they were so successful. But as problems of success usually are, this is a more difficult, at least a much more subtle, problem than any they tackled.[6]

Spread of Industrial Action

The spread of militant unionism to new groups of staff surprised managers in some organizations. Previously there were many managers, particularly in service organizations, who had never had to cope with the effects of industrial action. From the seventies on, many more managers in the UK have had to face this new disturbance to the smooth running of their departments and organizations. Strikes, overtime bans, working-to-rule and go-slows provide new needs for contingency planning to lessen their effects. The problem is intensified by organizations' vulnerability to action by small key groups of staff, particularly computer staff. Even if managers are lucky enough or able enough to avoid industrial action in their own organizations, they may still need to plan for the effects of industrial action taken elsewhere. An understanding of the causes of these actions, and the skill to prevent them where possible and to mitigate their effects where not, are requirements for the effective manager today.

6. Drucker, Peter F., *People and Performance*, op. cit., p. 24.

The Growth of Information Technology

Today managers need to understand how to use 'information technology' and the contributions that it can make to the solution of some of their problems. 'Information technology' is a general term for computers and other methods of handling information electronically. Computers can help managers' own work in different ways: by providing regular reports for monitoring what is happening, by greatly increasing managers' ability to ask for special information, and by making possible much more complicated analyses of what is happening or what might happen. Many questions can be answered now that could not have been answered before. Many strategic possibilities can be explored now that would have been too difficult before. But for much of this to be useful managers must know what questions to ask and be interested in asking them.

So far, at least, information technology has had a much less radical effect on the nature of middle and top management jobs than was being predicted in the late fifties. At that time Leavitt and Whisler wrote a much quoted article about management in the 1980s which argued that it would:

1. Move the boundary between planning and performance upward, so that many middle-management jobs would lose much of their discretionary elements as operating decisions were laid down governing day-to-day decisions.
2. Lead to a recentralization in large companies as top managers will take on even more of the planning and innovating functions.
3. Result in a reorganization of middle management with some jobs moving downwards in pay and prestige because they will require less discretion and skill, and others moving upwards into top management, because, like research and development, they become of increasing importance.
4. Make for a sharper line between top and middle management and one which is difficult to pass.[7]

7. Leavitt, Harold and Whisler, Thomas L., 'Management in the 1980s', *Harvard Business Review*, Vol. 36, No. 6, pp. 41–2, November/December 1958.

A study in the late sixties of the impact on management of different types of computer applications found that most of the effects on them were of little importance. A distinction was made between the effects of different types of application, as some impinge much more directly upon managers' jobs than others. One conclusion was that:

> Most of the effects of computer applications on management are not inevitable. The main exception is the automation of part or all of a small number of junior management jobs. The effects of the more advanced systems depend upon the use that managers make of the possibilities provided by the system, and upon whether they are stimulated to re-examine their policies or assumptions.[8]

Unfortunately there is no equivalent study for the mid-eighties, but it is clear that the Leavitt and Whisler predictions have not been realized. One reason for this is the dramatic changes in the nature of information technology, which have made personal computers possible and provided tools for middle managers as well as senior managers. Probably another reason is a change in many companies towards greater decentralization. Better information has helped to make that possible. Top management can now more quickly monitor what it wants to control and leave subordinates to run their profit centres. Yet another reason is that the software for many possible applications has lagged far behind the promises. Probably the most interesting reason for those who want to understand about managing is that many managers prefer to get their information from people. They do not know how to make the best use of the computer. This is more true for top managers than for middle managers. Some, but by no means all, middle managers do make substantial use of computers to provide them with the information that they want. Most top managers are not significant users. The jury is still out on whether they will become significant users. Some argue that they will as soon

8. Stewart, Rosemary, *How Computers Affect Management*, p. 220, Macmillan, London, 1971, and MIT, 1972.

as those who are familiar with computers and their potential reach top management posts. Others argue that computers can contribute little to top management.

Professor John Dearden took this view in an article in 1983. He argued that few top managers use the computing facilities that have been available for many years because they have a minimal interest in operations and spend little time on control information and numerical data. The computer in his view has not added to the important information required by top management.[9] Some top managers do find personal computers valuable as David Davis, senior executive of Tate and Lyle, PLC, pointed out in response to John Dearden.[10] He argued that they will become part of the furniture of senior managers' offices and will be used to ask important questions. All that is needed now, he says, for top managers to use them is the ability 'to think in a logical, organized manner'. A quite different reason for top managers to be interested in computers is that for some business information technology can be a strategic weapon. It can provide computer-based systems that increase the firm's productivity compared with their competitors, or, as for retail services like banking, provide new ways of providing services.

Managing Change

Resistance to Change

There are two main problems in the successful implementation of change: that the adjustments that are necessary may not be recognized or that they may be resisted. Good planning will help to prevent the first, but, if the change is to be successful, people at all levels in the company must make the necessary adjustments, and make them in time to avoid

9. Dearden, John, 'Will the Computer Change the Job of Top Management?', *Sloan Management Review (Forum)*, pp. 57–60, Fall, 1983.

10. Davis, David, 'Computers and Top Management', *Sloan Management Review (Forum)*, pp. 63–7, Spring 1984.

costly delays. A knowledge of the most common causes of resistance to change can be helpful for appreciating what opposition is likely to be met and why.

The place of one occupation in relation to others, in terms of remuneration, perks and prestige, may become established over the years. Rapid change frequently means a shift in the relative importance of occupations, the creation of new ones and the decline or even abolition of some old ones. Workers may resist a change because it affects their relative positions *vis-à-vis* other occupations, although in absolute terms they are no worse off.

Managers may be impatient with occupational resistance to change. They may feel that in a changing society the relative importance of different occupations is bound to change and that this is just something that people must adjust to. In particular, they may feel that if workers are protected from economic loss, they have no cause to complain; those who do are being unreasonable. In sum, they may be impatient – at such outmoded attitudes getting in the way of maximum productivity. But impatience is likely to do harm, especially if it makes them forget that much resistance to change is based on very solid reasons from the point of view of the affected individuals.

One of the most disturbing changes for individuals is that which reduces the value of their training and experience. This can happen when skill is replaced through mechanization or innovation, or when theoretical knowledge becomes more important than experience on the job. Employees may suffer economically through redundancy or lower earnings, or they may be economically protected but moved to a job that demands less skill and has a lower prestige. They may, particularly at the supervisory and managerial levels, remain in the same job but see their chances of promotion reduced by a change in the requirements for management jobs. Any change that reduces the value of employees' training and experience is likely to affect their sense of personal worth and their idea of their place in the company and in society. 'Tread softly because you tread on my dreams' might be amended, as a guide to those introducing change, to 'Tread softly because you tread on my sense of personal worth'. The prolonged coal strike in the UK in 1984 and early 1985 over the closure of uneconomic pits was but one, though a major, example of how strongly workers can feel about the loss of their way of life.

Resistance to change is often closely bound up with ideas of status. The status of people at any level may be threatened by change: the craftsman may become de-skilled; foremen may lose, indeed often already have lost, much of their authority; and the manager who has come up the hard way may have lower prestige than the graduate manager. Change may threaten status in three ways: by redundancy and unemployment, by moving an individual to a position of lower status, and by lowering the status of a person's present job. The latter often happens in some mergers, where the distance from 'the boss' becomes greater. Managers who are used to reporting to the managing director may feel a considerable loss of status if they then have to report to an intermediary manager.

Another social barrier to change is the attitude to mobility, which depends, in part, on the strength of local roots. The mobility of workers made redundant by the closure of engineering works in SE London during the period 1968–70 was studied by W. Daniel.[11] The five employers concerned in the closure were all able to offer redundant workers new jobs in locations to which they were transferring, but very few of the workers took them up. The most common reason given for not taking up the offers was that they wanted to continue living where they were (66 per cent). This answer was more common among semi-skilled workers (88 per cent) and declined with an increase in occupational level, being least common among managerial workers (56 per cent). Older employees were less willing to move. The overwhelming majority of reasons given for not wanting to move were related to family commitments, obligations and relationships. Daniel comments generally:

Case after case of closure and large-scale redundancy has revealed

11. Daniel, W. W., *Whatever Happened to the Workers in Woolwich*, PEP Broadsheet 537, July 1972.

a marked disinclination on the part of displaced workers to move to jobs outside their immediate journey to work areas; that is to say, to move to jobs which would involve them in moving house.[12]

These findings are broadly consistent with those for other countries.[13]

Employees may place a high value on their social relations both in the neighbourhood and at work. Changes that affect these may be resisted. A change to a shift system will have a profound effect on life outside work and may be disliked in consequence. Social relations at work may be upset by changing the people with whom they are used to working, by altering the size of the working group or the relations with their boss.

Resistance to change will be intensified by fear. This will come from the realistic fears for security that employees who have invested the best years of their life in an organization are bound to feel. There may also be personal anxieties, which may not be fully conscious and are aroused by anything that can be interpreted as a threat. The latter, especially, may account for the fact that even changes that improve earnings and conditions may be viewed, at least initially, with suspicion and fear.

Helping Adjustment to Change

Change, especially rapid change, is often upsetting. Management must recognize this if it is to ease adjustment to change. Even in changes that will be beneficial from the workers' point of view there will be a period while changing their habits when they will have to expend more physical and emotional energy than usual. Some research in America on perceived work pressure suggests that when this goes up, as it will during a change that means adapting to new methods

12. ibid., p. 113.
13. See, for example. Hunter, L. C. and Reid, G. L., *Urban Worker Mobility*, OECD, Paris, 1968.

of work, it affects workers' attitudes and leads to a drop in morale. At the least, change disturbs people's customary ways of doing things, which may make them fearful of what is going to happen to them. At the worst it deprives them of their livelihood and destroys the value of their years of training and experience. Thus, change is often painful and may cause social casualties. It is likely to be resisted, especially if it affects people's livelihood and way of life. But there is now enough evidence from experience and research to show that the pains of change can be reduced and that resistance may be overcome or prevented if enough trouble is taken.

The human aspects of change need as careful planning as the engineering or financial. Planning should cover both the likely human effects of the change and what can be done to lessen those that are harmful. This may be best done by appointing a manager to be responsible for trying to reduce the human problems of change. Other managers are likely to be too busy to give these problems the attention needed. There are two aspects to managing change: planning and individual counselling. The planning should include a study of how a drop in the number of employees can, as far as possible, be achieved without compulsory redundancy, by provision for early retirement, careful plans for retraining that are adapted to the needs of different employees, protection against a drop in earnings during the retraining period, and help in getting another job. The timing and method of announcing the changes should also be well planned. Everything possible should be done to reduce the fear that comes from uncertainty and misapprehension. Such fear is likely to be the first effect of many changes. Individual counselling can do much to allay fears and to help people to understand and to assess what options are open to them.

Changes that affect the composition of working groups need special attention. Managers should never forget in their enthusiasm for planning the technical aspect of changes that many changes in the organization of work have effects on people. Many studies show that in designing work organization more attention needs to be given to social factors if the best results are to be obtained in productivity and workers' satisfaction.

When management is planning changes in the organization of work, it should consider if it can do the following: increase the content of the job, provide more overlapping of work within the individual work group, give the group greater responsibility, and encourage the supervisor to emphasize the technical and advisory aspect of the job. In sum, to give the individual groups greater responsibility for the work in which all can share, rather than each having a small self-contained job.[14]

Research on change shows that those who are likely to be affected by it should be told of what is planned and be consulted about what should be done, so that they have a say in how and when the changes that will affect them are introduced. The classic study of the value of involving workers in the process of change was carried out by Coch and French in a sewing factory employing about 600 people. The workers were paid by piece rates based on time study. In the past the firm had met strong resistance when it changed production schedules and methods; during the changeover periods production dropped, immediately and markedly, and frequently did not recover completely. There was also a high labour turnover and generally low morale. The experiment consisted of adopting a different method of introducing the change in each of three groups. The first group used the traditional method, in which top management issued an instruction to make the change and the workers and their immediate supervisors did not participate in the planning. The second group participated in the plan through representatives. In the third all members participated. Production dropped initially in all groups, but much less in the third one. It also recovered much more rapidly in this group. The first, or non-participation, group showed no significant improvement of production during the first forty days after the changeover. During this time 17 per cent of the group left,

14. What has been learnt about job design is discussed at length in Chapter 2 of *The Reality Of Organizations*.

compared with none in the other two groups. The first group also complained about the payment system and about individual managers, complaints which were not made by the other groups.[15]

Two examples of changes in the office both show careful planning for the change but differ radically in their way of deciding what should be done. In the first management investigated and decided. In the second the decision of what should be done came out of a study carried out by the secretaries. The first example is of what one large firm did when it decided to introduce word processing at its London headquarters.[16] It made the following studies in preparation for the change:

1. A detailed calculation of the full costs of employing typists, including all overhead costs, to explore the relative benefits of increased productivity against higher employment.
2. A detailed study of the costs of labour turnover.
3. A workstudy of the average typist's day, including identification of paper handling, error rates and idle time, to identify potential productivity gains.
4. An attitude survey to establish typists' likes and dislikes with a view to reducing labour turnover and an assessment of the costs involved.
5. A survey of available word processing systems.

The chosen system led to a productivity increase of 200 per cent and a reduced rate of turnover, and it achieved financial breakeven earlier than anticipated. But there were some disadvantages: the rearrangement of work into centralized typing pools reduced the level of support for some personnel, and a decision to separate printing from typing caused some friction.

15. Coch, L. and French, J. R. P., 'Overcoming Resistance to Change', *Human Relations*, Vol. I, pp. 512–32. Tavistock Publications, London, 1948.

16. Nahapiet, Janine, 'Assessing the Potential Costs and Benefit of New Office Technology', Templeton College, Management Research Papers, 84/4, pp. 16–17.

The problem is that a cost–benefit analysis ignores social factors and is unsuitable for dealing with the complexity of working relationships. When technology is changed, work often has to be redesigned.

An alternative approach was tried by ICI in 1978.[17] This is a study of how a group of secretaries in ICI's Central Management Services Department designed a new, efficient and satisfying work system for themselves. They used a design methodology that went under the acronym ETHICS: Effective Technical and Human Design of Computerbased Systems.

The group of secretaries started work on this project in 1978. At that time they had two word processors, which they liked but which were not used very efficiently. Managers felt a more effective service could be provided. The secretaries examined two areas: what created job satisfaction and what ICI needed in terms of service. They investigated what other ICI divisions and other firms did with word processors. They arranged a demonstration for their managers so that the managers would understand the capabilities and constraints of the new technology. One important feature of the design process was cooperation not only between the secretaries and their managers but also with top management, who could provide guidelines on company policy and could boost morale.

The immediate gain for the secretaries was a greater ability to concentrate on those parts of their job that gave them most satisfaction; and for ICI the more efficient and effective use of both capital equipment – the word processor – and human resources – the secretaries. The longer-term gain was the creation of a group capable of helping with the introduction of new communications and information technology – for instance, electronic mail. The ICI example is one of many studies that show the advantages of engaging those affected by the change in its design.

Changes at any level can cause problems, not just those on

17. Mumford, Enid, 'Designing Secretaries', *Manchester Business School Monograph*, MBS, 1983.

the shop floor or in the office. The effects of rapid change on the organization of management can be far-reaching and, unless this is realized, it may result in inefficiency as well as frustration and strain. Rapid change increases the need for frequent personal contact between managers. Managers' jobs become more fluid, so that they cannot be set down in detailed job descriptions or prescribed by rules. The status that goes with the job may also become more indefinite. Managers will be judged at least in part by how they show up in the frequent discussions made necessary by change and under the pressure resulting from it.

Managers who fear uncertainty will feel insecure under the constant challenge of fluid rather than structured or prescribed relations. If the company is one where management rivalries are intense, rapid change may intensify them, as managers will no longer be able to retreat to their own defined jobs for protection – or if they seek to do so, as they may, so much the worse for the success of the change.

Managing changes well is difficult but some clear lessons can be drawn from the results of research over the years. Do try to prevent unnecessary anxiety about what is going to happen. Do bring those likely to be affected by the change into the planning of what should be done. People are much more willing to accept, and to make work, something they help to create. Do not blame the troubles that arise on personal cussedness; they may contribute, but there are deeper causes. Do constantly re-examine what the organization is supposed to be doing and how it is doing it, with the aim of adopting whatever seem the most appropriate methods and structure. Do emphasize common tasks, both for the organization as a whole and for the individual groups, rather than separate jobs. Finally, do seek to encourage an atmosphere in which cooperative relations can flourish, rather than one in which people seek to score points or to assert prestige. The greater the change, the more important become human relations in determining its success or failure; hence the greater the need for the manager to understand human resistance to change.

SUMMARY

Managers need to look outside their organization much more than they had to in the past. They must understand what aspects of their environment – political, economic, technical and social – both in their own country and abroad are likely to affect the problems they face. They must try to influence the environment where they can. They must learn to plan contingently and to adapt to the unforeseen.

Change, to be successful, must be carefully planned. Such planning must also include the likely human effects of the change and what can be done to ease adjustment to them. In such planning, managers can benefit from a knowledge of the most common causes of resistance to change. One of the greatest is fear. Much of it may be unnecessary and result from uncertainty and misapprehension. Some of it may be a reflection of the individual's unconscious fears triggered off by what is seen as a threat to security.

Resistance to change often comes from social barriers, of which the most important are the rigidities between occupations. Change may destroy a long-established relation between occupations. For the individual this can mean a loss in the value of training and experience, and with them a decline in status. Therefore, resistance to change is often bound up with the ideas of status. Another social barrier to change is the attitude to mobility. Many British workers are reluctant to move their homes, although more are willing to change their occupations.

There is sufficient evidence to show that much can be done to reduce resistance to change at all levels. Careful planning and consultation with the workers, or their representatives, on details of the plan which affect them can do a great deal to enlist the workers' cooperation. The same is true for those who need to make changes at any level. People are likely to support what they help to create.

Rapid change can transform the nature of the manager's job, making it more fluid in terms of both responsibilities and status. Successful managers will learn to live with, and to enjoy, the uncertainties that this will cause. They will be ready to search for the methods and the structure that are most suitable to the company's situation. When things go wrong, they will look for causes rather than finding scape-goats. Above all, they will see change as an opportunity for cooperative and questioning endeavour.

Part IV

Managing Now and in the Future

11

Practical Implications

This chapter summarizes for the manager the practical implications of the previous chapters. It offers help in identifying and coping with the most common problems of management. Such problems remain whatever changes take place. The end of the chapter reviews the ways in which the task of managing may change the working lifetime of the reader.

Managing Now: Becoming a Better Manager

Managers' jobs differ greatly, but there are some common aspects to being an effective manager. The manager has to learn to manage himself or herself. Any manager who is in charge of other people has to learn how to get their commitment. All managers have to work with people other than their subordinates and have to learn the skills required to get their cooperation. Managers need to be thinking how to improve the efficiency of the operation for which they are responsible. This includes managing resources efficiently: particularly people, materials and equipment. Managers also need to be alert to the threats and opportunities that affect the unit for which they are responsible, whether it is a section, department, factory, hospital or company. The nearer they are to the top of an organization, the more essential it is for them to think strategically about the future.

Managers who went to improve should review both their effectiveness and their efficiency. Effectiveness is doing the right things. Efficiency is making the most economical use of the resources. Effectiveness is more important than efficiency, because one must be doing the right kind of work. Only then does it matter whether the work is done efficiently.

Managing Oneself

Learning to Trust Other People

This is one of the hardest lessons for new managers to learn: some never learn it. It is natural for many managers to find it difficult to trust others. They may have been promoted because they are more energetic and more efficient than the other people with whom they work. They may be correct in thinking that they would do a job better than their subordinate, but it may not be an effective use of their time to do so. Managing is getting things done through other people. A manager who thinks about what can be done only in terms of what he or she can do cannot be effective. Managing is not a solo activity, although some managers talk as if they depend solely upon themselves.

Managers must learn to accept their dependence upon other people. A key part of being a good manager is managing that dependence. Managers who say that they cannot delegate because they have poor subordinates may genuinely be unfortunate in the calibre of the subordinates that they have inherited or been given. More often this view is a criticism of themselves: a criticism either of their unwillingness to delegate when they could and should do so, or a criticism of their selection, training and development of their subordinates. The comment by Levinson is a useful warning: 'the successful executive is critical of his own performance; the unsuccessful of the performance of others'.[1]

1. Levinson, Harry, *The Exceptional Executive*, p. 254, Harvard University Press, Cambridge, Mass., 1968.

Understanding One's own Strengths and Weaknesses

Such knowledge is an essential part of being a good manager – a knowledge that should improve as one grows older and hopefully becomes more mature. Managers need to understand their own strengths of character, outlook, knowledge and skills. They need, even more, to recognize their weaknesses and limitations. Weaknesses of character are perhaps more easily recognized than limitation of outlook. We all see the world through our own eyes, and what we notice and what we do not notice is distinctive. Self-knowledge can help one to assess what one can contribute and what is needed to complement the distinctive character of that contribution. Personality tests and assessment centres can help in this understanding. The Myers Briggs personality test, based upon the theories of Jung, is a useful tool for managers who wish to understand how they perceive and judge the world, and which sides of their personality they have developed most.[2]

Two examples of how senior managers described what they thought to be their strengths and weaknesses may be helpful to readers in trying to review their own. The first manager described his strengths as follows: 'I rarely get irritated. I am single-minded so that if I see something that needs doing it will get done. I am technically competent. I have the ability to consult and to listen though I don't believe in committee decisions. I am practical: I always ask "Will it work?"' He also said that he regarded his dogmatism as a strength because it meant that he was willing to say what he believed even if he was the only one to speak out. He thought that his main weakness was that he was a driver not a leader. He also lacked confidence, so that he started by thinking that others would do better than he would, though this did have the advantage of making him put in more effort.

The other manager saw his strengths as follows: 'I am highly stress resistant. I am responsive to new ideas. I am an extremely good decision-maker because I am willing to take

2. Myers, Isabel Briggs, *The Myers-Briggs Type Indicator*, Consulting Psychologists Press, Palo Alto, California, 1962.

decisions when they are, as most are, finely balanced, rather than to opt out by asking for more information. I get on well with people and am good at leading. I have a sense of humour and commonsense.' This collection of very desirable managerial virtues was balanced by an awareness of weakness. He described his weakness as follows: 'I am not a natural delegator because I think that I can do it better and faster and am egotistical. I am too willing to sacrifice myself and others to the company. I don't suffer fools gladly and switch off too visibly if I am bored.' Weaknesses, he thought, were often the opposite of strengths – a remark that is a useful guide to understanding one's own weaknesses.

Coping with Stress

An aspect of understanding oneself is being able to recognize one's own personal symptoms of stress. Each of us has our own warning signs that we have been pushing ourselves too hard. Indigestion, sleeping badly, irritability and excessive tiredness are common warning signs that should not be ignored. The danger is that the more overtired one gets, the more one may feel indispensable. Indeed, such a feeling is in itself a warning sign. Peter Nixon, a consultant cardiologist at Charing Cross Hospital, provides a useful diagram of the relation between the amount of stimulus and the level of performance. See 'The Human Function Curve' opposite. It shows that for a time being keyed up increases one's level of performance, but that there comes a point where this is more than one can take and one's performance begins to decline. If this is not recognized, people will continue to go downhill and be liable to a heart attack. The solution, Dr Nixon argues, is not drugs to suppress the symptoms but learning ways of backing off so as to reduce the extent to which one is keyed up. Managers need, if they are to continue to be effective under stressful conditions, to learn how to relax. When somebody is already fully stretched, relaxation will not be found in stressful pursuits like competitive sports. Such pastimes are for those who are still on the up curve of the diagram.

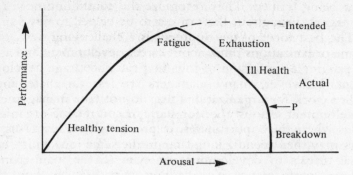

P — The point at which even minimal arousal may precipitate a breakdown

Source: Nixon, P. G. F., The Human Function Curve: with special reference to cardiovascular disorders, *Practitioner*, 1976, 217, 765, 935.

Many people are more prone to stress at some stages of their life than at others. The mid-life crisis is widely talked about as the main period of stress, but there are different cycles throughout life with periods of re-examination, anxiety and stress. Individuals who understand these stages can recognize what is happening and be better able to cope with them. The brief bibliography at the back lists a few books that managers have found helpful in understanding and trying to manage their careers. They point out that a career must be seen in relation to stages in family life.

Self-development

Self-development is now recognized as an essential aspect of management development. Others may try to promote one's development through management education or a different kind of job, but whether one does develop depends upon oneself. There is a danger for all of us that as we grow older we become less able to adapt to change. There is another danger that we develop tunnel vision, so that our view of what can be done, and of possible solutions to problems is too narrow. In some organizations this danger is recognized.

IBM, for example, expects all its managers to spend a week a year being trained. They recognize the continuing need for managers throughout their career to be helped to develop.

The best form of development is a challenging new job. Some organizations think about career development and aim to provide a succession of jobs that can encourage development. However, many managers are less fortunate: they either work for organizations that do not take management development seriously, or for static or contracting organizations where the opportunities for promotion are low. Managers may then spend a long time in the same job, which can pose threats to development or even to the maintenance of one's performance. The diagram on p. 193 was about the desirability of an optimum amount of stimulus for performance. Where the job is not providing enough stimulus, one needs to search out other ways of remaining interested and alert or try hard to change one's job.

Many managers' jobs are very busy, so that managers must necessarily spend a lot of their time, and can too easily spend all their time, relying on the habits that they have developed. Self-development means trying to avoid being set in a mould of thinking and acting.

Effective Use of Time

Many managers would have put this first because it is the need that is most commonly recognized by those managers who wish to improve their effectiveness. It is not put first here because it is not the most important aspect of becoming a better manager. A good programme on the use of executive time can help managers to use their time more economically, but it cannot ensure that they are doing the right things. The distinction between the effective and the efficient use of time should be recognized. To improve the first, managers must decide what they personally ought to be doing. To improve the second, they can learn to organize their time better. Some people will find that one of the commercial time management systems helps them to do so. The utility of such systems depends upon the individual's temperament.

A very useful exercise for all managers is to keep a record of what they do in detail for a week or longer.[3] This can remove illusions about what one actually does. Many managers find that their picture of how they spend their time is different from what they really do. It is useful to check this out at intervals. A diary can help one to appraise the distribution of one's time between different aspects of the job and between different people. Both the content of what one is doing and the pattern of the day can be assessed. Was there, for example, any time during the week when one worked alone and uninterrupted for any useful period of time? If not, would it be desirable to make such time? Nobody can make time if they believe that they are indispensable, and must therefore be always available. Many managers have found that they can use their time better if they consider who they need to be available to and when. Regular meetings with subordinates are often a better use both of their time and of yours than an open door policy. They can mean that you take time to discuss problems together, rather than just have frequent brief and fragmented interchanges.

Moral Stamina

This is a different kind of heading from the previous ones, though it could be seen as an aspect of self-development. Because managing means working with other people, there are many opportunities for moral cowardice. The temptation to be liked and to be seen as a nice person may make the manager unwilling to talk frankly with subordinates or with colleagues. Managing other people necessarily means making judgements about them and at times taking difficult and sometimes painful decisions affecting them. A lesson that some managers have learned, sometimes too late, is that many people would prefer greater frankness about how they are doing and what are their career prospects than their boss thinks that they can accept.

Managers have a duty to help subordinates to develop their

3. Stewart, Rosemary, *Managers and Their Jobs*, op. cit., Chapter 8, 'Lessons for the Manager' provides some examples.

own moral stamina. Drucker puts this well: 'A manager: Directs people or misdirects them; Brings out what is in them or stifles them; Strengthens their integrity or corrupts them; Trains them to stand upright and strong or deforms them.'[4]

Managing Others

Managers necessarily work with and through other people, but who they have to work with and how difficult this is varies in different jobs.[5] The difficulty and importance of managing one's subordinates successfully varies considerably in different jobs. In some this is the main aspect of the job, in others relations with one's boss or bosses, with colleagues or with people outside the organization, may be much more important. The main problems in working successfully with other people are discussed below, though some will be much more important in some jobs than in others.

Enlisting Commitment

The more common word is 'motivation': the phrase 'enlisting commitment' is used instead because it highlights what is needed. In Chapter 3 we traced the history of some panaceas that managers had thought would solve the problem for them. The history showed that there were no panaceas, but that what matters is the right attitude to people. This means accepting that most people want to do a good day's work but need a favourable setting in which to do it. Small groups and small establishments provide a better setting than large ones. People need to be involved if they are to be interested, and if they are to accept change. They need to be trusted if they are to behave responsibly.

Building and Maintaining a Team

A team can be defined as a group of people who pull together like a team of horses. The process of team-building is not easy. It requires the right mix of people, a task to which they

4. Drucker, Peter, *People and Performances*, op. cit., p. 55.
5. These differences are discussed in Stewart, Rosemary, *Contrasts in Management*, op. cit.

can become committed, and one which is in the organization's interest. There are a number of different roles that need to be performed in a team if it is to work effectively. Hence, when recruiting a new person to a management group, one should think of what personal skills are missing to make the group more effective.

Many managers who move companies often take some people with them. They may have chosen people who complement them and built up a new team whom they trust. They know that they will be more effective in their new job if they are supported by people who already form an effective managerial team. Good managers know that a group of people who have become a team will achieve far more than those who have not.

Living with Touchiness

Employees are, and must be treated as, adults, but adults are touchy – some adults more so than others. Those who have remained married will have learnt what things upset their spouse and thus how to avoid some marital quarrels. Sensitivity to other people's feelings will help to avoid many otherwise unexpected problems. People vary in how they react, but yet there are some useful guidelines. Probably most important is that many people mind about their status, which should be recognized in making any changes. Managers should ask themselves 'In what ways could this change be seen as adversely affecting anyone's status?' Such preliminary thought can help to prevent difficulties later; some people are more status-conscious than others and are, therefore, more easily upset.

Trading Successfully

Some managers will know at once what this heading means, but others may be perplexed. 'Trading' is one way of describing a balance of favours. For example, young couples in a housing estate may establish a baby-sitting group. It may be formalized so that a record is kept of who has sat for whom and how often, or it may be informal. Either way,

some account will be taken of the exchange relationship.
Many managers have to rely on colleagues in other departments or on people outside the organization if they are to get
their work done. Such cooperation may depend at least in
part upon the trading of favours. The formal organization
can help to ensure the necessary cooperation but it is unlikely
to make trading unnecessary. In some jobs it is easy – people
want what you have to offer and are willing to give you what
you need – but in others it is more difficult. You may be
offering a service that is not widely accepted, you may want
help that is costly for others to give. Managers who have
to deal with people in other departments need to recognize
where a trading relation exists and what they have to trade.

Trading relations exist both inside and outside the organization. The number of the latter are increasing as more
services are being bought in from outside. Managers outside
the purchasing department are likely to buy such services.
As Leonard Sayles pointed out as long ago as 1964, 'Many
employment relationships are being converted into contrac-
tual relationships: these require "trading" ability more than
traditional "leadership"'.[6] The trade is often not a purely
financial one. Accountants and other service providers may
be willing to work for you, and work for you well, for a
variety of reasons other than pay. The reasons can be very
varied. One may be the prestige of your organization: suppliers may be pleased to quote you as one of their customers.
The interest of the work can be a major incentive for some
service providers, particularly academics and computer consultants. The ambience of your organization and whether
others enjoy working for you often matters, too. Good managers should know what are their trading counters with
particular individuals.

Network-building

Increasingly managers require a wide range of contacts.
There are still jobs with a limited and specified set of people

6. Sayles, Leonard, *Managerial Behaviour*, op. cit., p. 65.

with whom to work, but many jobs now require contacts in other departments at different levels and with a variety of people outside the organization. John Kotter, in his study of fifteen general managers in the US, was struck by the amount of time that they spent establishing a network of cooperative relations. This was a major activity during the first six months in a new job. These networks often included hundreds, even thousands, of individuals. Their typical network was so large that he was unable to draw it in any detail.[7] Leonard Sayles in his earlier study of engineering managers had found the same thing although on a smaller scale. Increasingly many managers behave and need to behave like journalists in their cultivation of contacts. This means getting to know a wide range of people and keeping these contacts warm. The more senior the manager, the more important is a good network – 'good' meaning wide-ranging, friendly and informed in the areas where the manager may need help. 'Help' can range from finding another job to providing a service that is needed, suggesting a good candidate for a vacancy, or knowing who can help with a particular problem. Some managers are natural network-builders. Others may need to learn the importance of developing a supportive network.

Improvement Projects

Good managers are not only trying to maintain the status quo and cope with the problems and changes that come at them, they are also trying to improve things. When one is new in a job, it may be easy to see improvements that one thinks need making – inefficiencies that one's predecessor had not noticed or did not think were important – hence the expression 'new broom'. When a manager has been in a job for some time, it is easy to fall into a familiar pattern even if it is mainly one of crisis-handling. Some managers who have been in the same job for some time still keep alive their belief that improvements are both possible and necessary. One way

7. Kotter, John, *The General Managers*, op. cit., p. 67.

of translating such a belief into action is to set oneself improvement projects with objectives and measurable targets to a timescale. Some improvements can be effected in this formal way; others may have to be pursued more informally. Trying to change people's attitudes may mean looking for opportunities that will help to effect the change. A good manager both plans improvements and is on the alert for opportunities to promote change. A manager who thinks that no more improvements are possible, or necessary, should quickly try to find another job!

Managing the Environment

This rather grand phrase applies to managers whose jobs and departments and companies are adversely affected by what is happening outside the organization. Nowadays more and more managers have contacts outside the organization; some of those who do not could and should have. 'Managing the environment' means that managers should not just be trying to react successfully to the adverse changes that come from outside the organization, they should be trying to prevent or moderate such changes. The organization's environment includes government, competitors, customers, suppliers of goods, services and people and the community. 'Government' for firms trading overseas means foreign as well as home government. Local government can be an important influence, too.

Managers can often make the environment more favourable to themselves. This is true for many managers, not just those at the top. A simple example is cultivating the local schools so as to try to ensure a supply of good school leavers. Another is getting to know relevant academics who may be able to help with a problem or interest a student in working on it. Cultivating politicians both at the national and local level is one way by which managers can try to get advance warning of changes that may be likely to affect them and try to influence what changes do take place. Taking care to be seen as a good neighbour by the local community can help to prevent trouble in the future. The aim should be to establish a good reputation among the groups whose goodwill is important. Cultivating the relevant people is part of the network-building that many managers should be doing.

Managing in the Future

No one can know for certain what managing in the future will be like. We can be almost sure that there will be major unforeseen changes. Current changes provide some guide to the future. These changes are briefly discussed below.

Who has to be Managed?

What it is like to manage is changing because the people to be managed have changed, and so has their relation to the manager. There is a continuing major shift in employment from manufacturing to service industries. Thus there are many fewer manual workers to be managed and far more people who are providing a service. Generally managers will be responsible for smaller groups of better educated staff.

Managers are now, and increasingly in the future will be, spending more of their time with people who are not their subordinates, and often may not be a fellow employee. Managing then becomes trying to enlist the cooperation of people in other departments or of suppliers or consultants outside the organization. These are trading relations rather than ones determined by the boss–subordinate hierarchy.

Anyway the boss–subordinate hierarchy has changed. Authority is, and is likely to continue to be, less acceptable than in the past. This reflects a major change in society: what has been termed the end of the grateful society. Better educated and more independent people expect to be consulted rather than to be told what to do.

A more recent change is the decline in the number of people employed in an organization because of sub-contracting some services. This change seems likely to accelerate. Competitive pressures make the search for ways of improving efficiency more important. For some services, information technology also makes it much easier. Indeed, a new term, 'networking', has been coined for people who can work from home and be linked by computer terminal to the organization for which they are working. Such work may be paid for by a retainer or a fee rather than by a full-time salary; the former employee may also be expected to find other contractors.

What has to be Managed?

Increasingly the answer is 'information' rather than physical resources: information about money, people and goods, information about targets and whether they are being met, information about possibilities and which are the more likely. Managers will increasingly have to know how to manage information in the sense of knowing what information they want and how to use what they receive. The danger is information overload making the manager's job harder.

Another answer is 'relationships'. This answer is implicit in the description of the changes in who has to be managed. Organizations, and hence managers, are much more exposed than in the past to a variety of interest groups. Managers have to try to establish good relations with those outside the organization whose goodwill can be important: national and local politicians, consumers, community groups and educationalists.

The Managerial Career

Short, fragmented and anxious might be the pessimist's prediction. 'Short', because the trend towards early retirement, at least from one's main employer, seems likely to continue. 'Fragmented', because more managers will have to change employers and may have spells of unemployment in between. 'Anxious', because of the greater insecurity and competitive pressures, improved performance monitoring and the stress from trying to cope with rapid change.

Challenging, fulfilling, varied and liberated might be the optimist's prediction. The first three because managers are likely to have more responsibility, greater variety, be called upon to manage a much wider range of people and to cope with more rapid change. 'Liberated', because they will not feel tied to one employer for life but will be able to change employers more easily, to start their own business or work on a fee basis from home. More managers will cease to be managers and start different careers.

Selected Bibliography
for Managers

There are now, happily, a number of good general books by social scientists that managers can find helpful and readable. Not all are included in this short list. The ones given here are those that managers, from a wide variety of organizations, attending programmes at Templeton College have said they found helpful. Different people find different books relevant to them, so do not be discouraged if one does not appeal.

BARTOLOME, FERNANDO and EVANS, PAUL, *Must Success Cost So Much?*, Grant McIntyre, London, 1980.
   A book that should make any ambitious executive think whether he or she has the right priorities between work and private life.
BROWN, PAUL L., *Managing Behavior on the Job*, Wiley, New York, 1982.
   A consultant's book stressing the need to pinpoint unsatisfactory behaviour, with specific examples of how to analyse it, its antecedents and consequences and how to change them. A useful book for people problems.
DRUCKER, PETER F., *The Effective Executive*, Heinemann, London, 1966.
   Illustrates one main theme: build on people's strengths.

DRUCKER, PETER, *The Practice of Management*, Pan, 1984, first published by Heinemann, 1955, 479 pp.
Lengthy, but lively, interesting and full of examples – mainly American. Drucker's best, a general book about management.

FOX, ALAN, *Man Mismanagement*, Hutchinson, London, 1974, 179 pp.
A thought-provoking analysis of the reasons for the problems in management–worker relations and suggestions for their remedy.

HANDY, CHARLES, *Understanding Organizations*, Penguin, Harmondsworth, Second edition, 1981, 473 pp.
Emphasizes diagnostic skills in understanding behaviour in organizations, good examples and summaries of research.

JUDSON, A. S., *Manager's Guide to Making Changes*, Wiley, London, 1966, 181 pp.
Perhaps the most helpful book on the subject, particularly easy to read.

LEAVITT, HAROLD J., *Managerial Psychology, An Introduction to Individuals, Pairs and Groups in Organizations*, University of Chicago, Chicago and London, Fourth edition, 1978, 385 pp.
Focuses more on the individual and on small groups than the other books. A classic with wide appeal.

McGREGOR, DOUGLAS, *The Human Side of Enterprise*, McGraw-Hill, New York (London, 1960), 246 pp.
Describes the now famous Theory X and Theory Y of people's attitude to work.

OWEN, TREVOR, *Making Organizations Work*, Martinus Nijhoff, Leiden, 1978.
A highly personal approach on the theme that managerial energy needs releasing and effectively using.

PETERS, THOMAS J. and WATERMAN ROBERT H., JR., *In Search of Excellence: Lessons from America's Best-Run Companies*, Harper and Row, New York, 1982.
The American best-seller which presents many well-known lessons, and some less well-known, in a vivid style. It epitomizes the interest in improving the culture of one's organization.

SCHEIN, E. H., *Career Dynamics*, Addison Wesley, Mass., 1978.
Useful for managers wanting to review their careers.

STEWART, ROSEMARY, *The Reality of Organizations*, Macmillan, London; Pan, Second edition, 1986.

Companion volume to this one.

STEWART, VALERIE and ANDREW, *Managing the Manager's Growth*, Gower, Aldershot, 1978, 257 pp.

An unusually helpful book about how to develop managers.

STEWART, VALERIE and ANDREW, *Managing the Poor Performer*, Gower, Aldershot, 1982.

Useful analysis and suggestions for action.

Index